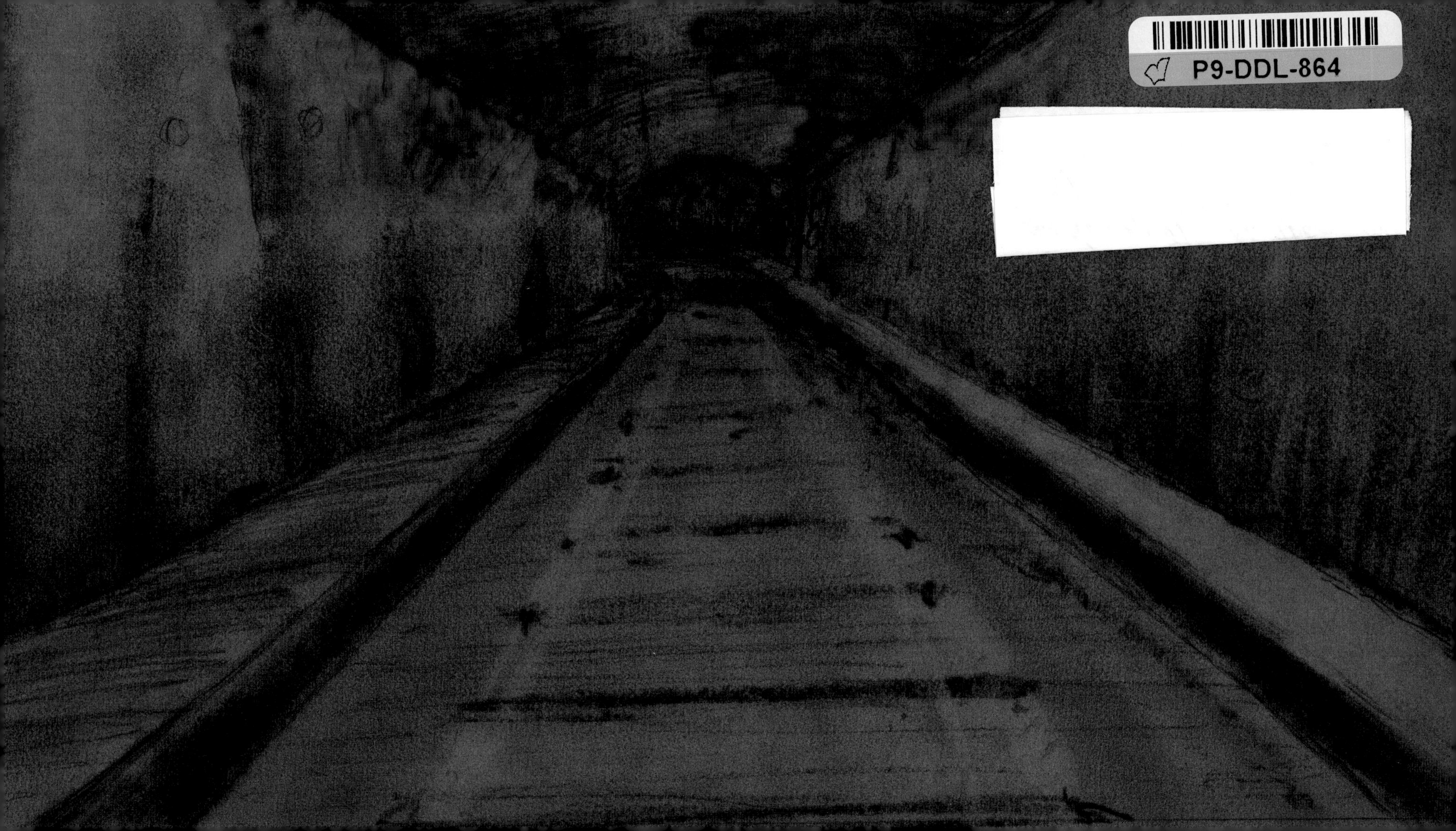

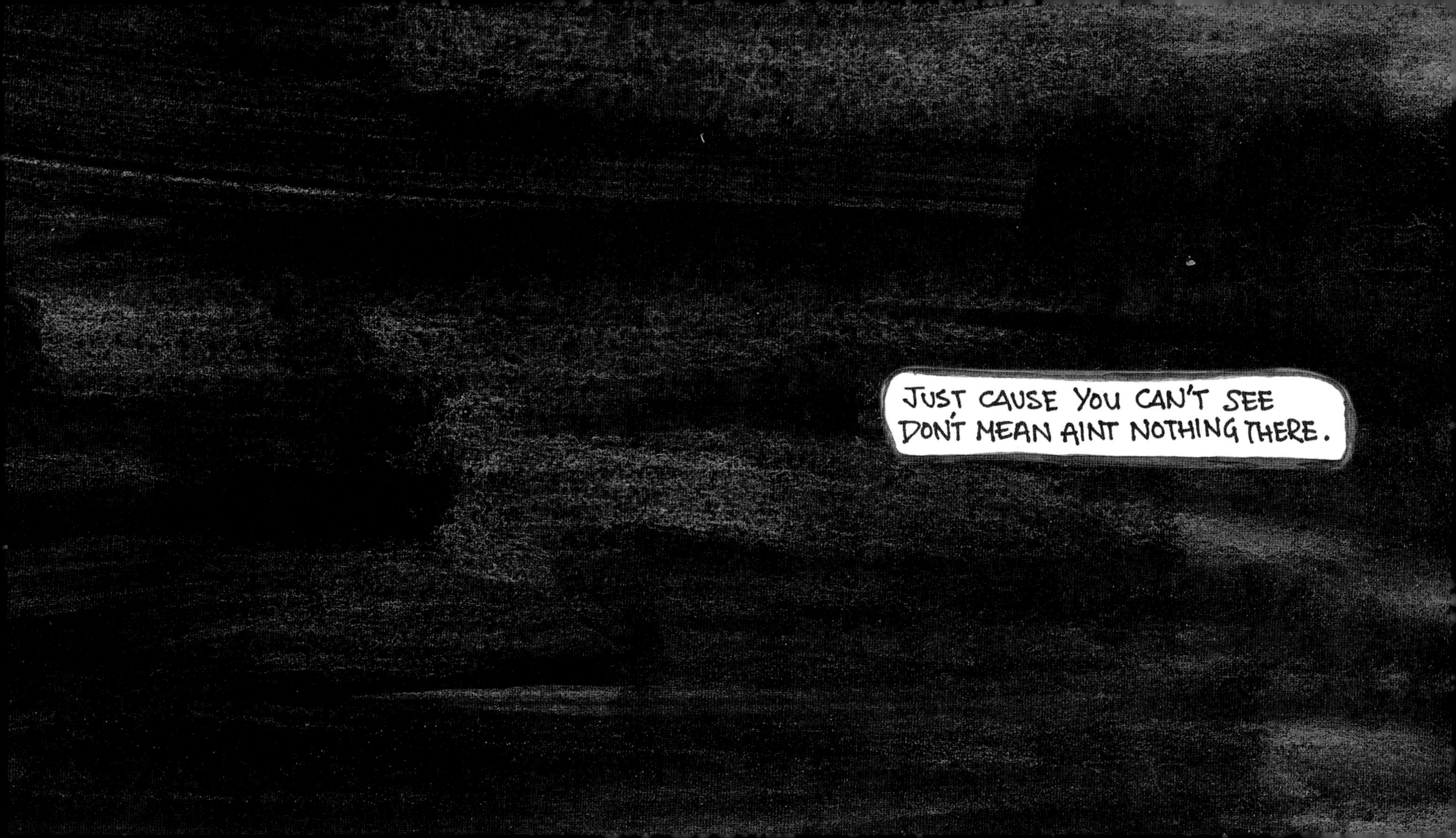
JUST CAUSE YOU CAN'T SEE DON'T MEAN AINT NOTHING THERE.

PITCH BLACK

DON'T BE SKERD

YOUME LANDOWNE
and
ANTHONY HORTON

CINCO PUNTOS PRESS

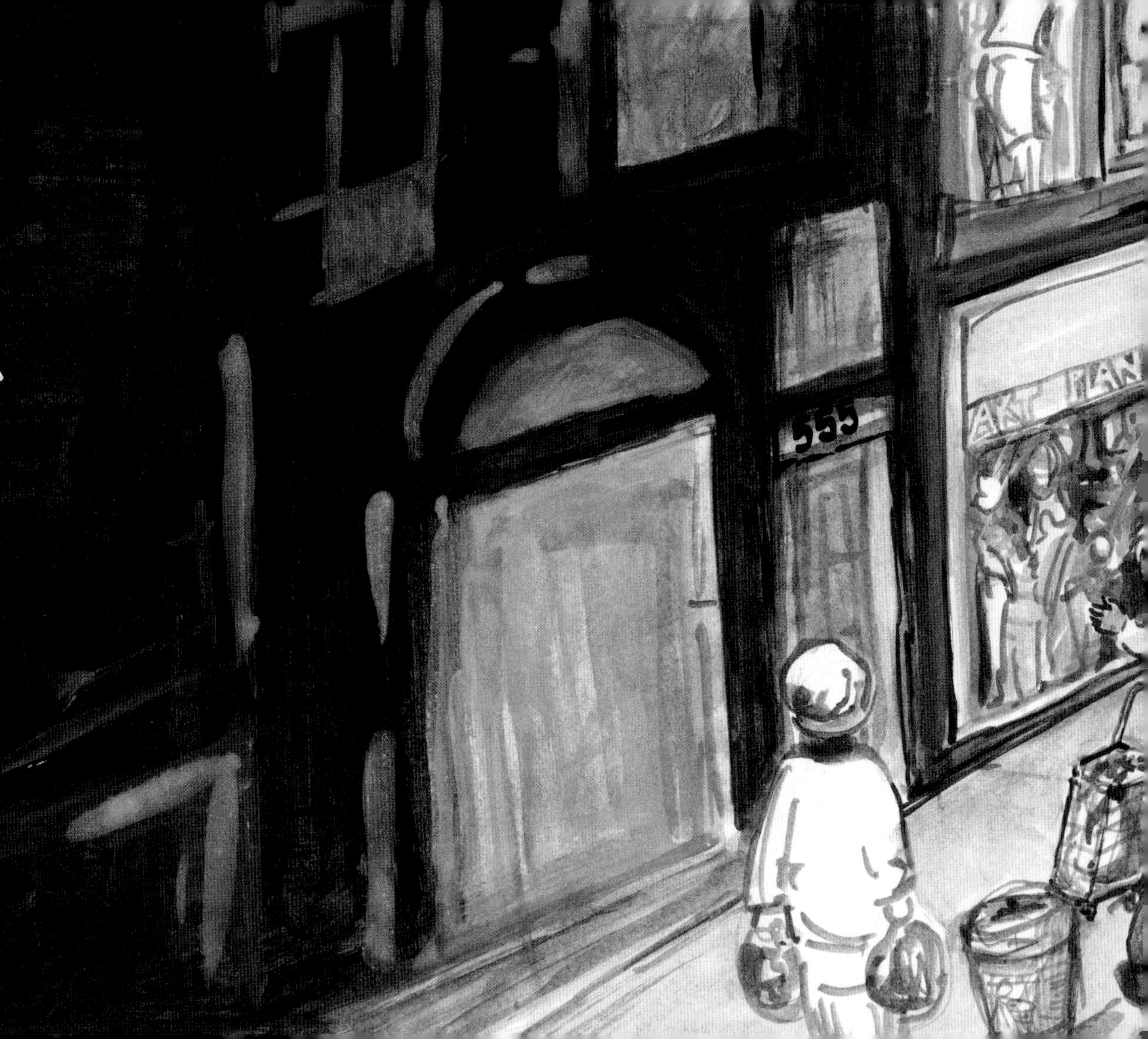
555
ART

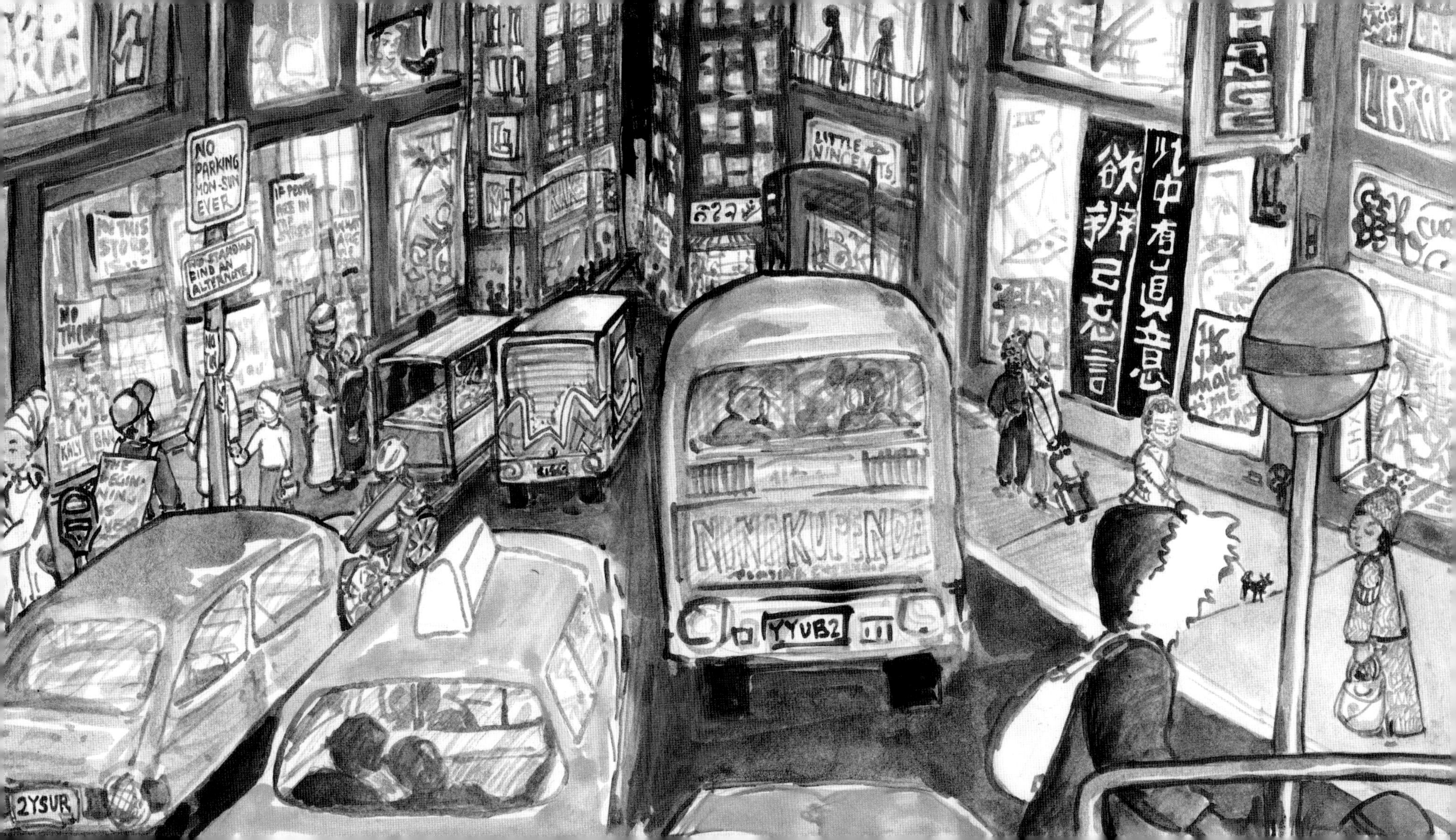
NO PARKING MON-SUN EVER
NO STANDING FIND AN ALTERNATE
此中有真意
欲辨已忘言
NINI KUPENDA
YYUB2
2YSUR

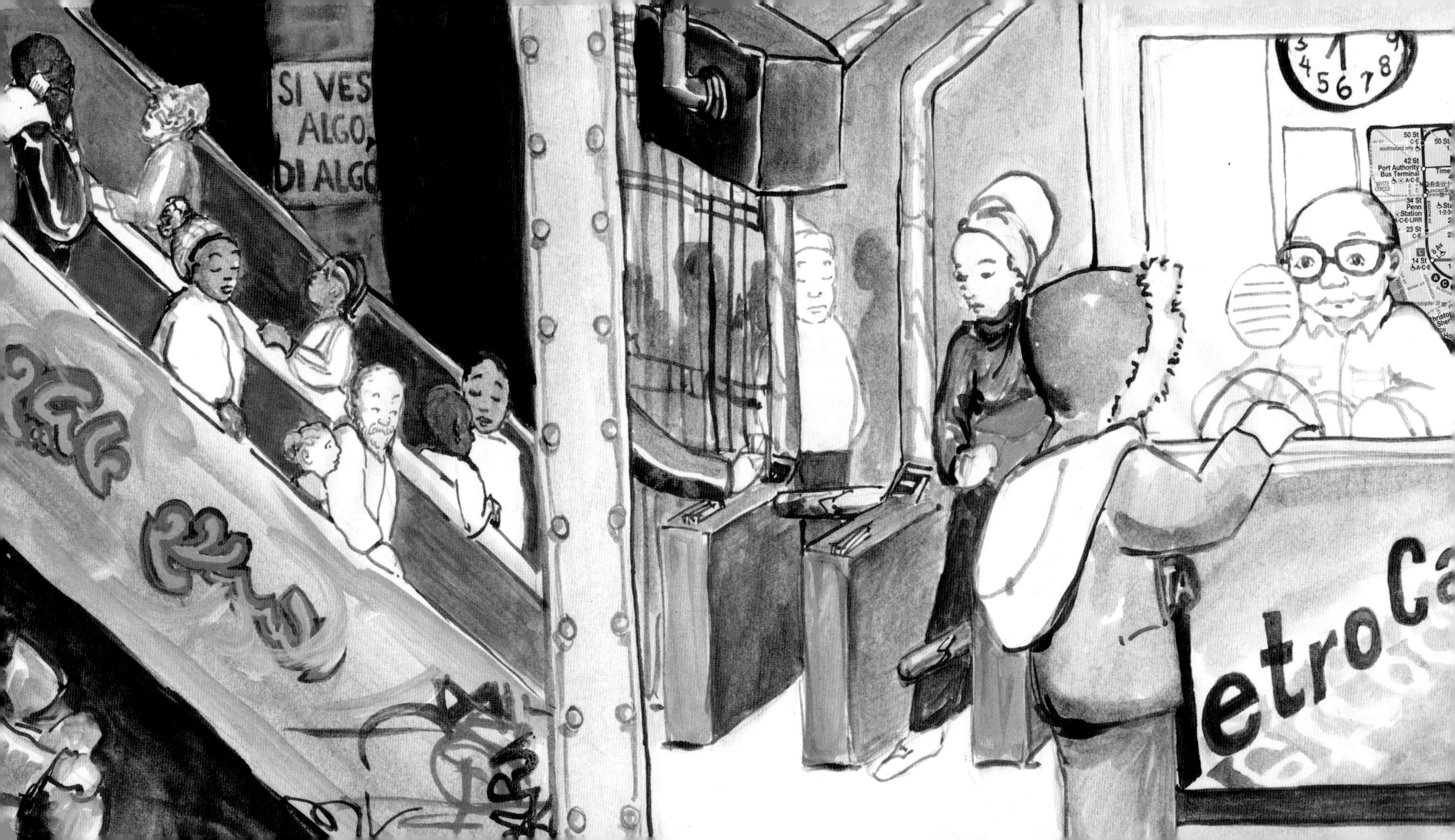
SI VES
ALGO,
DI ALGO
50 St
42 St
Port Authority
Bus Terminal
34 St
Penn
Station
23 St
14 St
etroCa

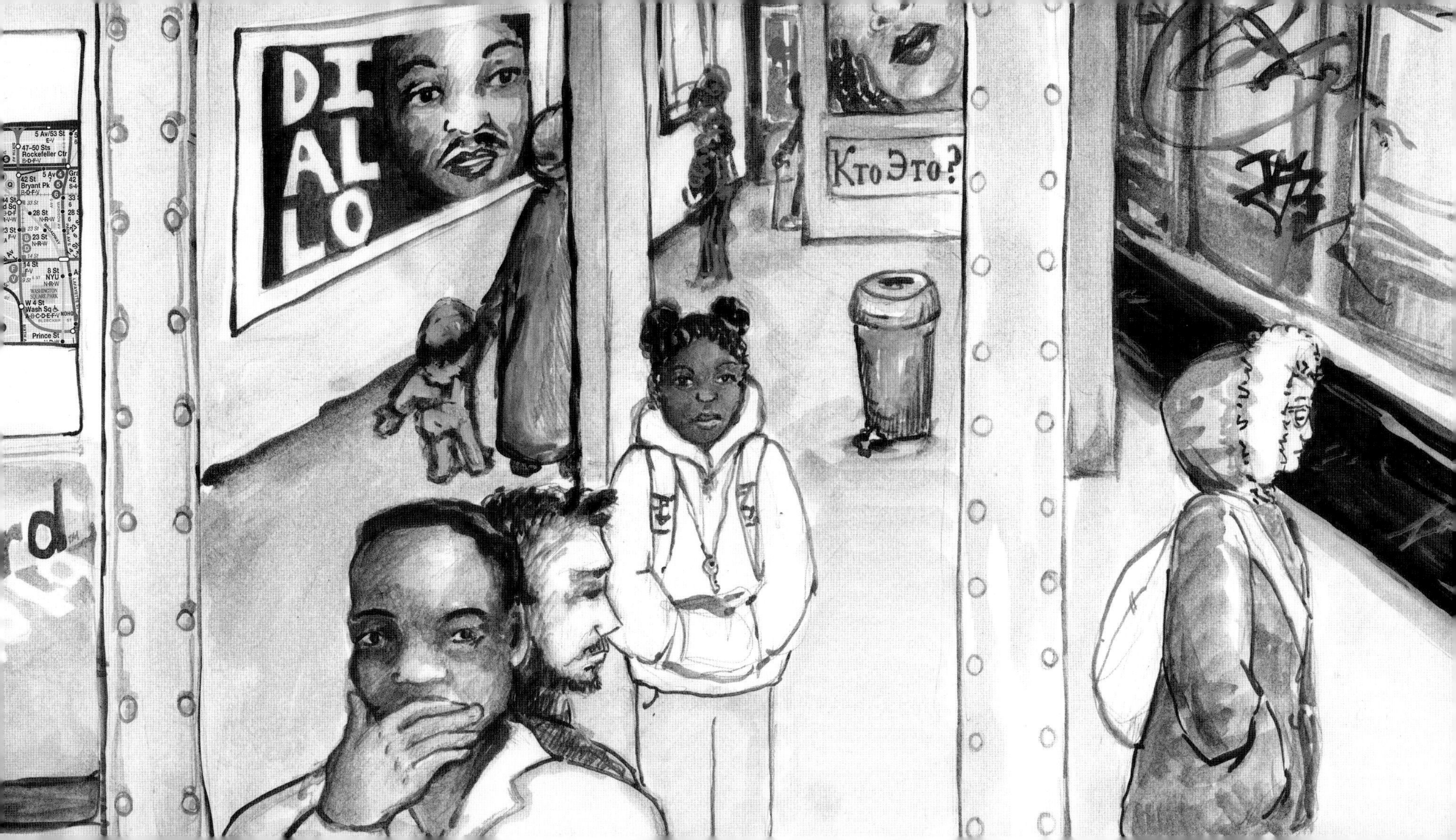
DI
AL
LO
Кто Это?
5 Av/53 St
47-50 Sts
Rockefeller Ctr
Bryant Pk
42 St
28 St
23 St
14 St
8 St
NYU
W 4 St
Wash Sq
WASHINGTON SQUARE PARK
Prince St
rd

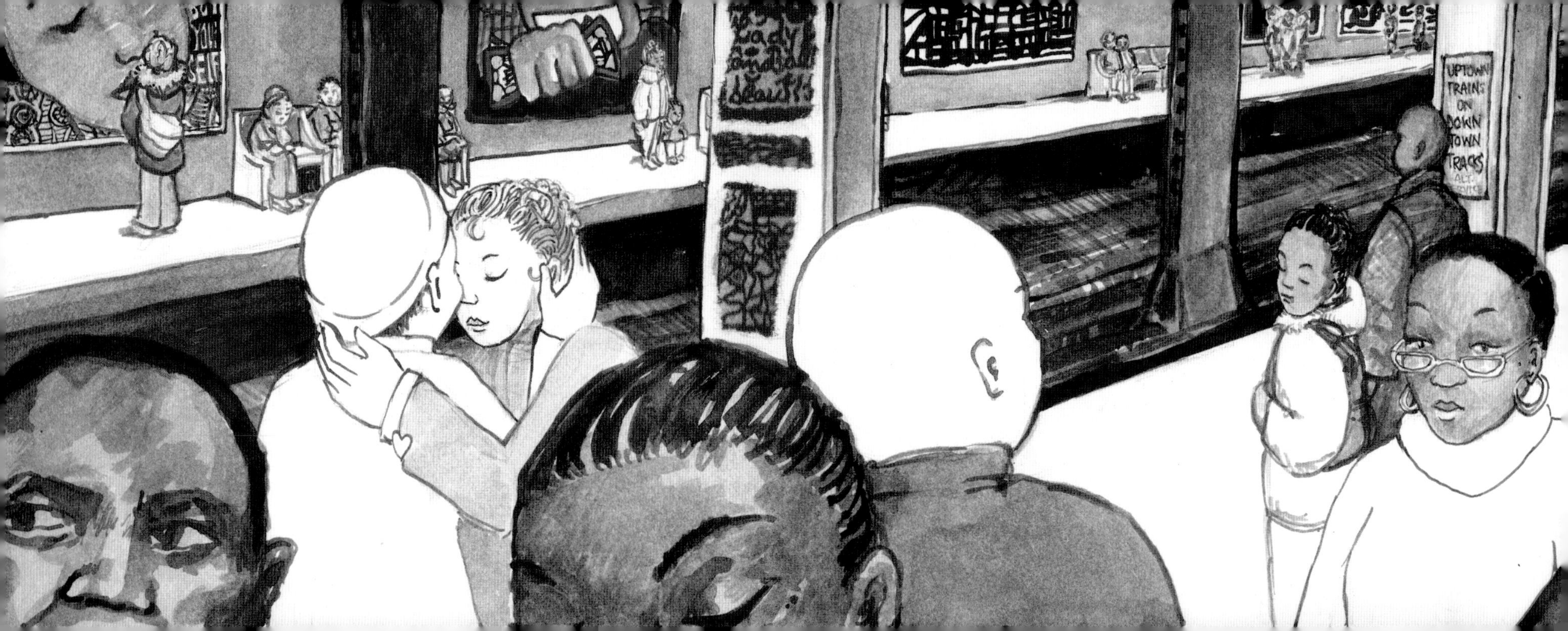
UPTOWN TRAINS ON DOWNTOWN TRACKS

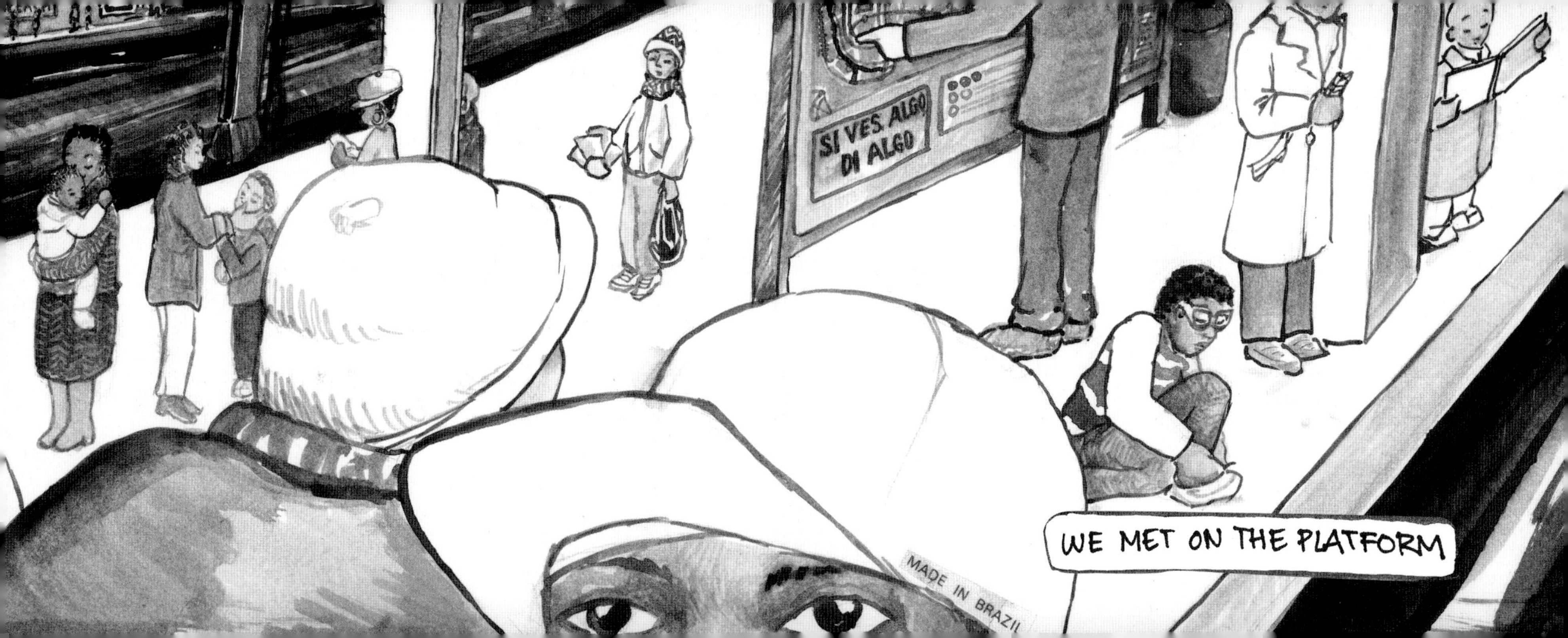
SI VES ALGO
DI ALGO
MADE IN BRAZIL
WE MET ON THE PLATFORM

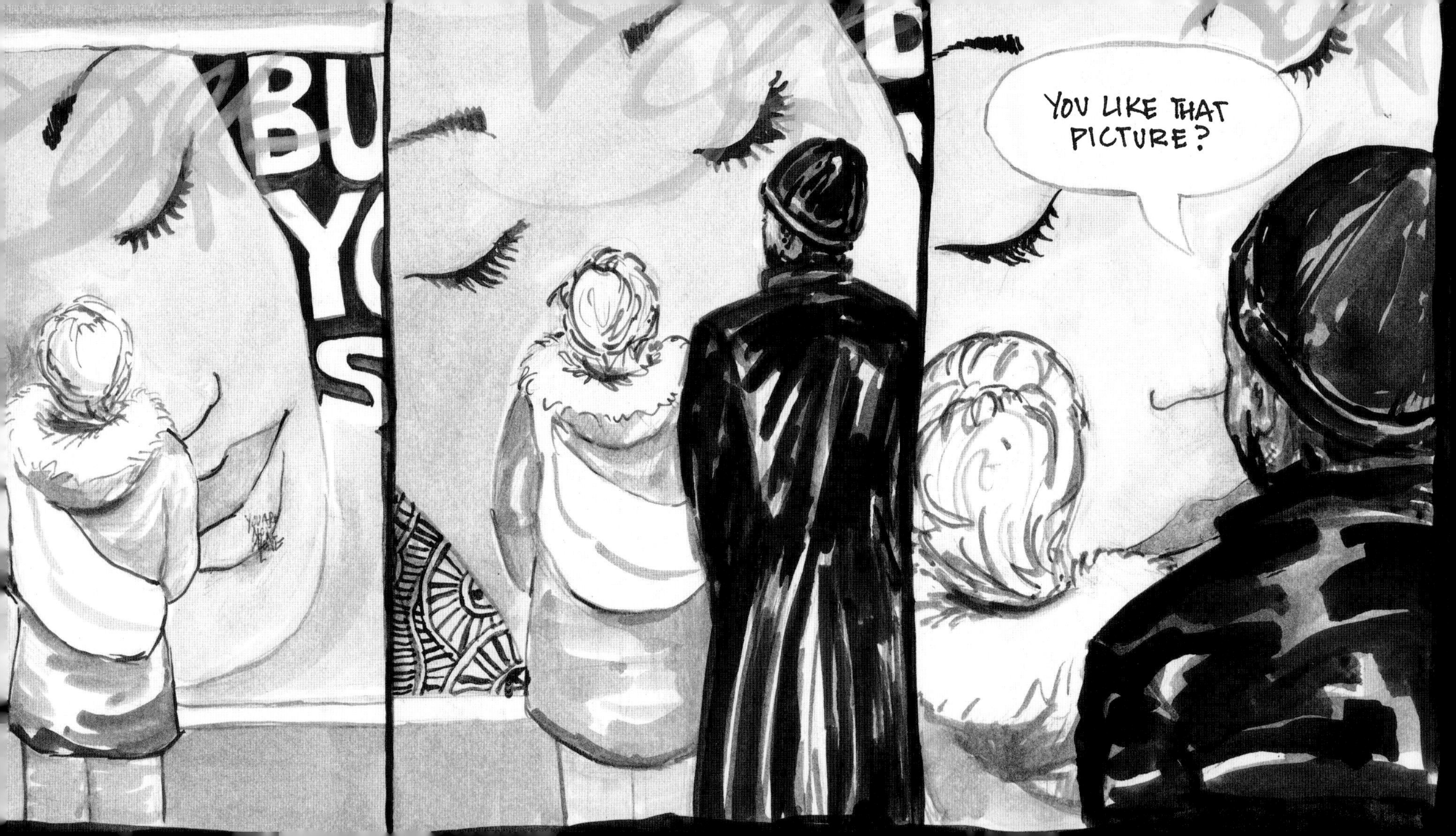
YOU LIKE THAT PICTURE?

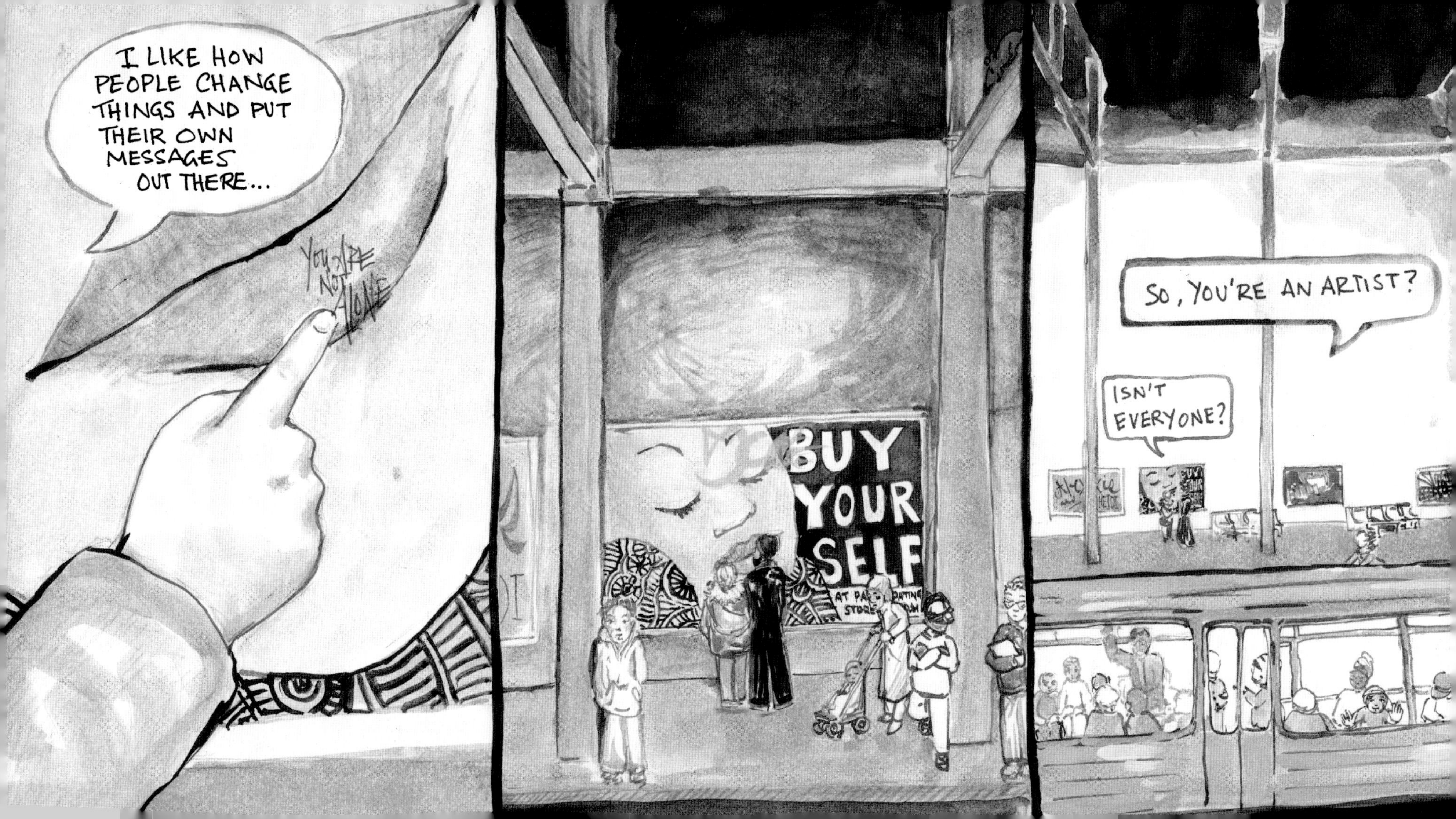
I LIKE HOW PEOPLE CHANGE THINGS AND PUT THEIR OWN MESSAGES OUT THERE...
YOU ARE NOT ALONE
BUY YOUR SELF
SO, YOU'RE AN ARTIST?
ISN'T EVERYONE?

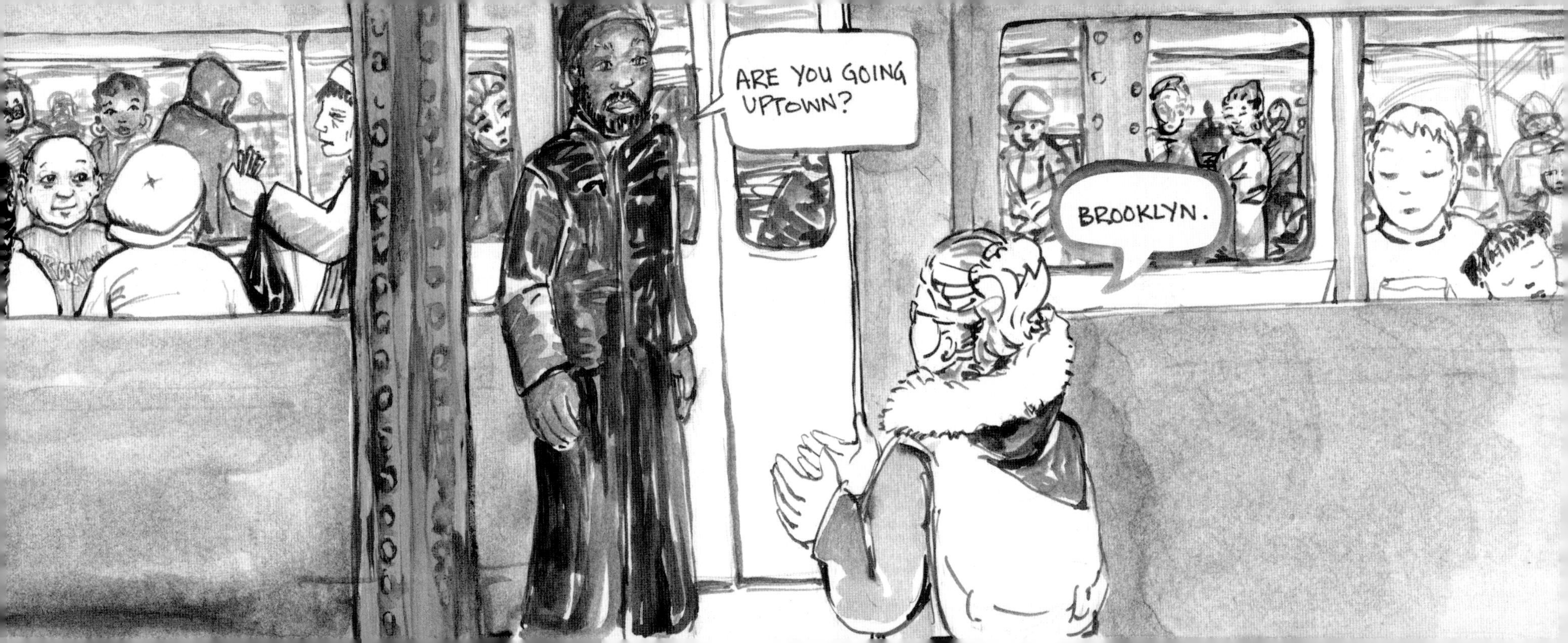
ARE YOU GOING UPTOWN?
BROOKLYN.

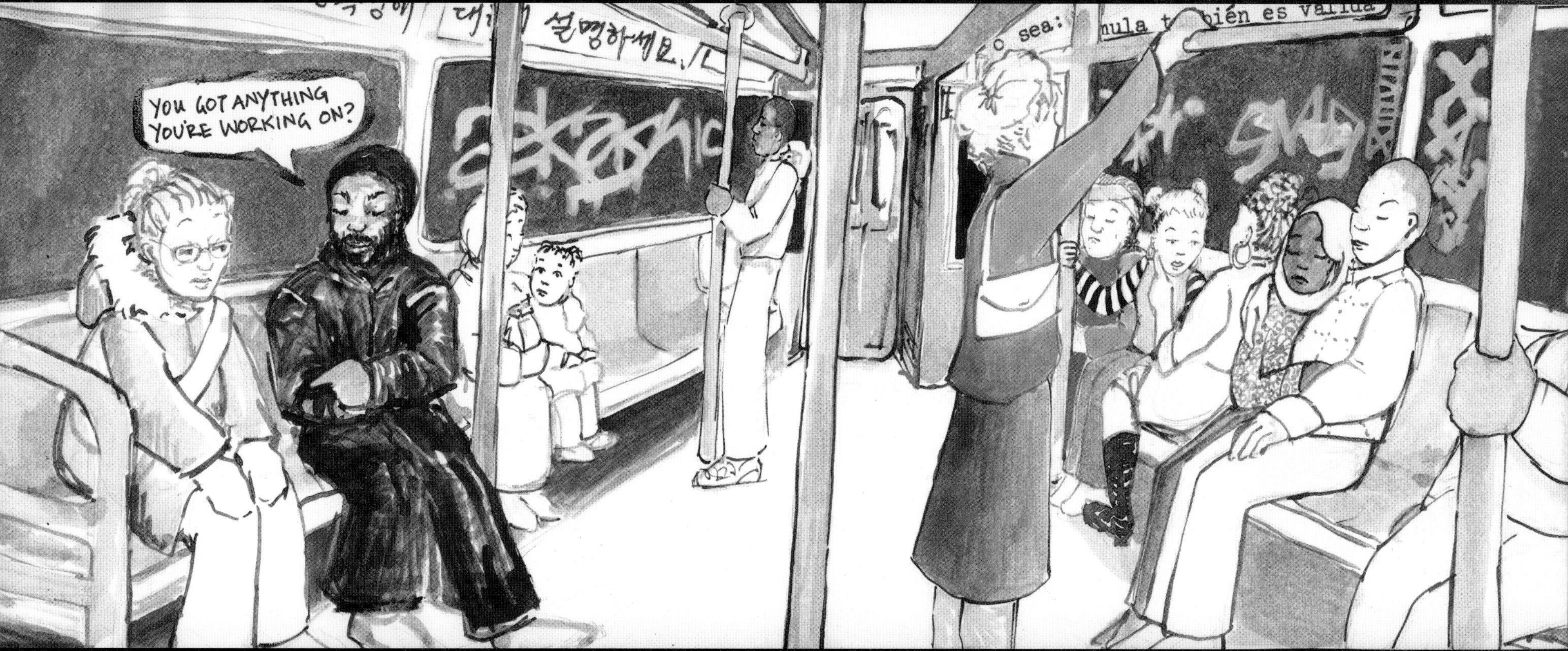
YOU GOT ANYTHING YOU'RE WORKING ON?

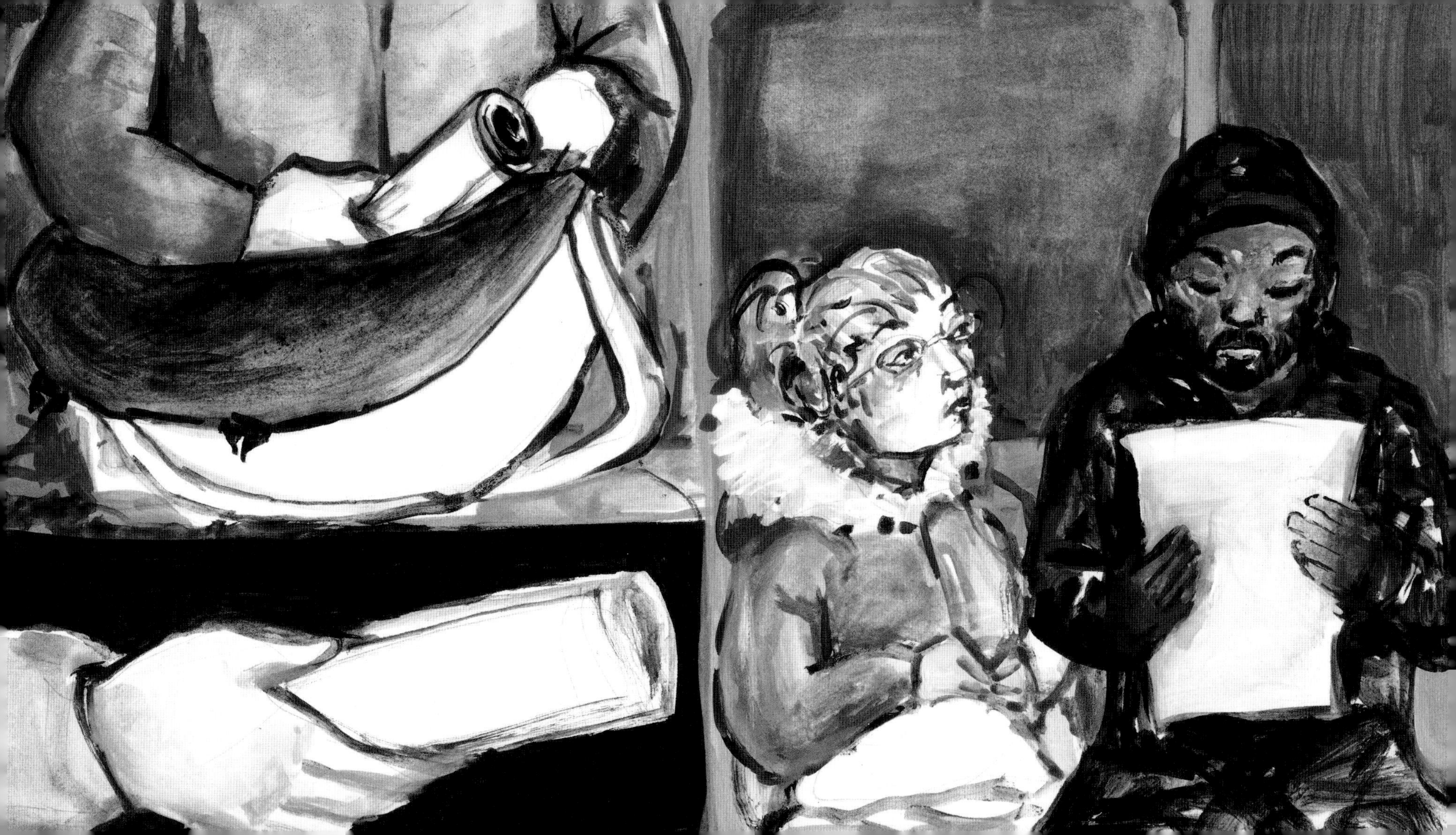

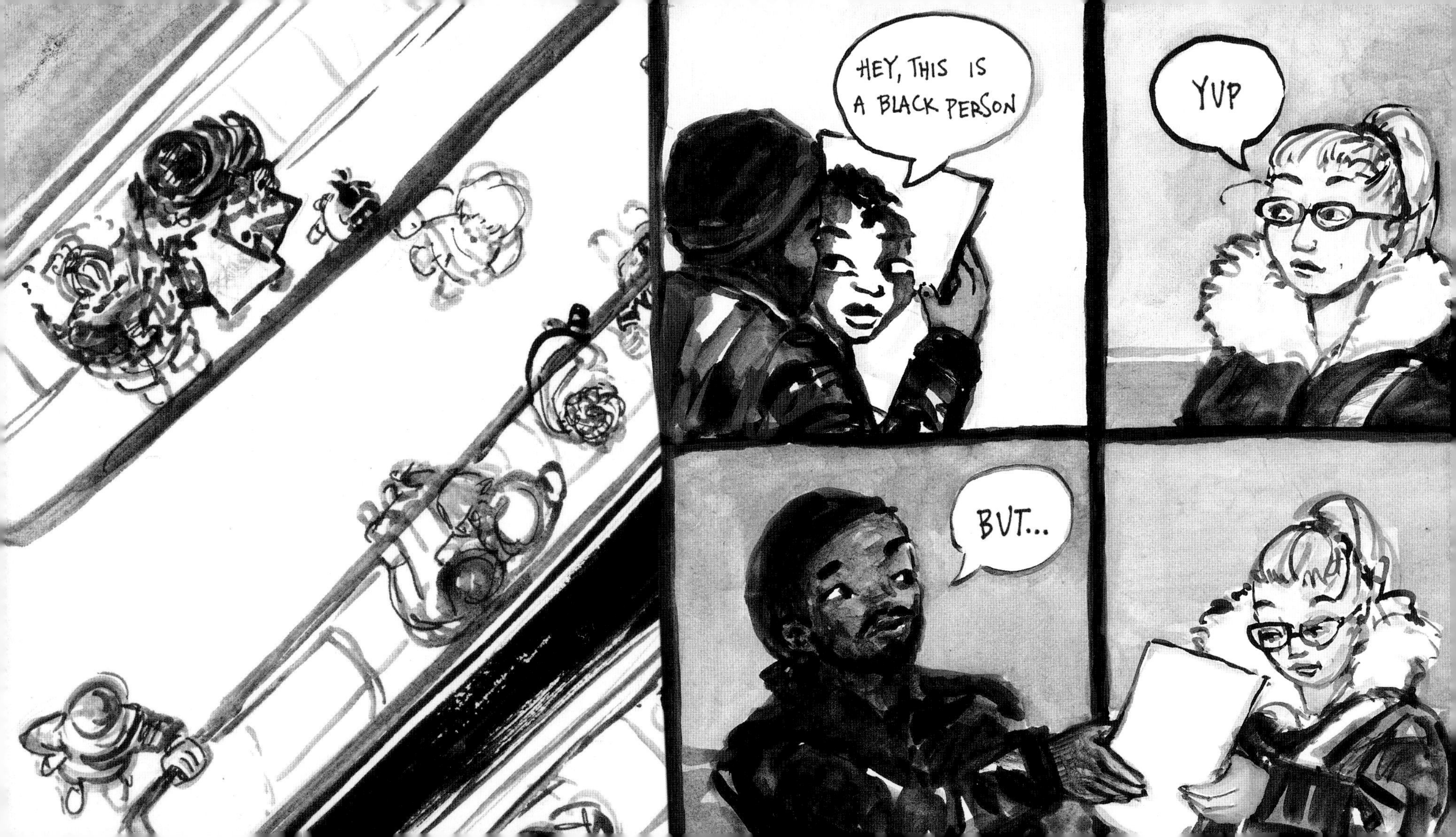
HEY, THIS IS A BLACK PERSON
YUP
BUT...

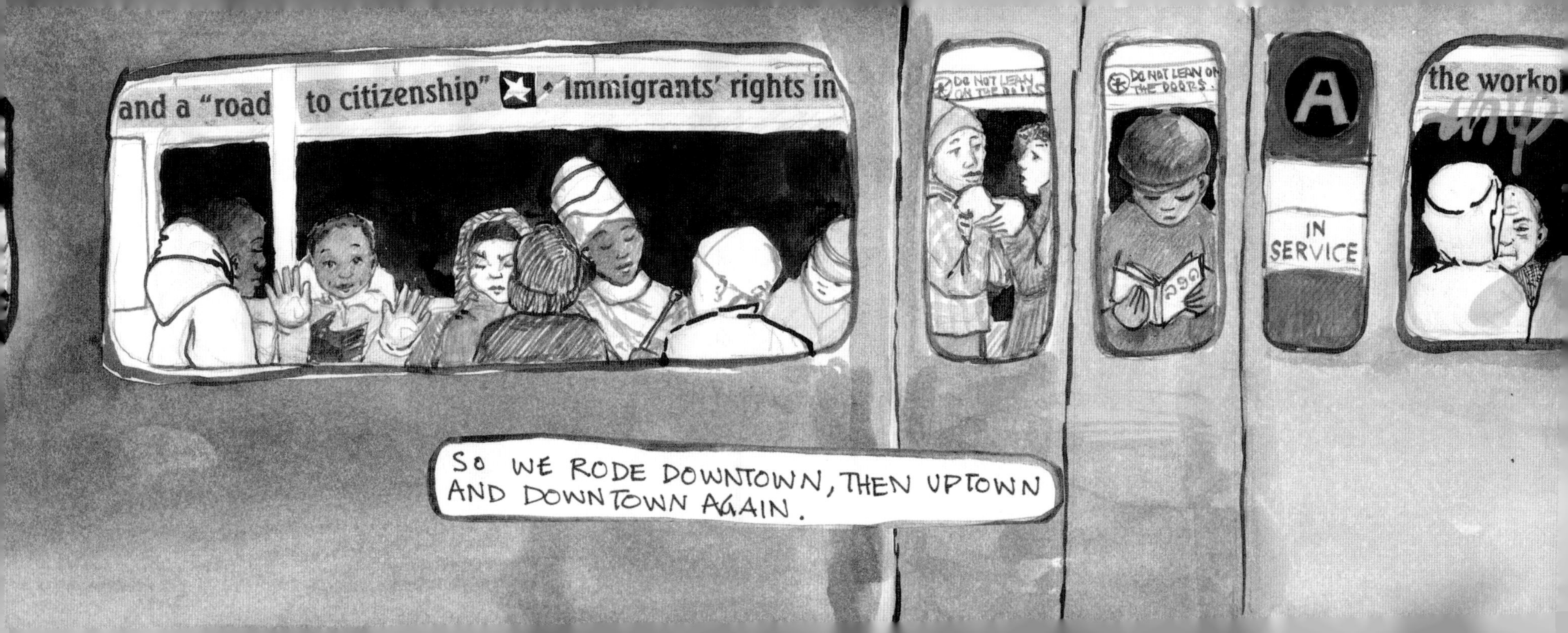
and a "road to citizenship" ★ • immigrants' rights in
DO NOT LEAN ON THE DOORS
DO NOT LEAN ON THE DOORS.
A
IN SERVICE
the workpl
SO WE RODE DOWNTOWN, THEN UPTOWN AND DOWNTOWN AGAIN.

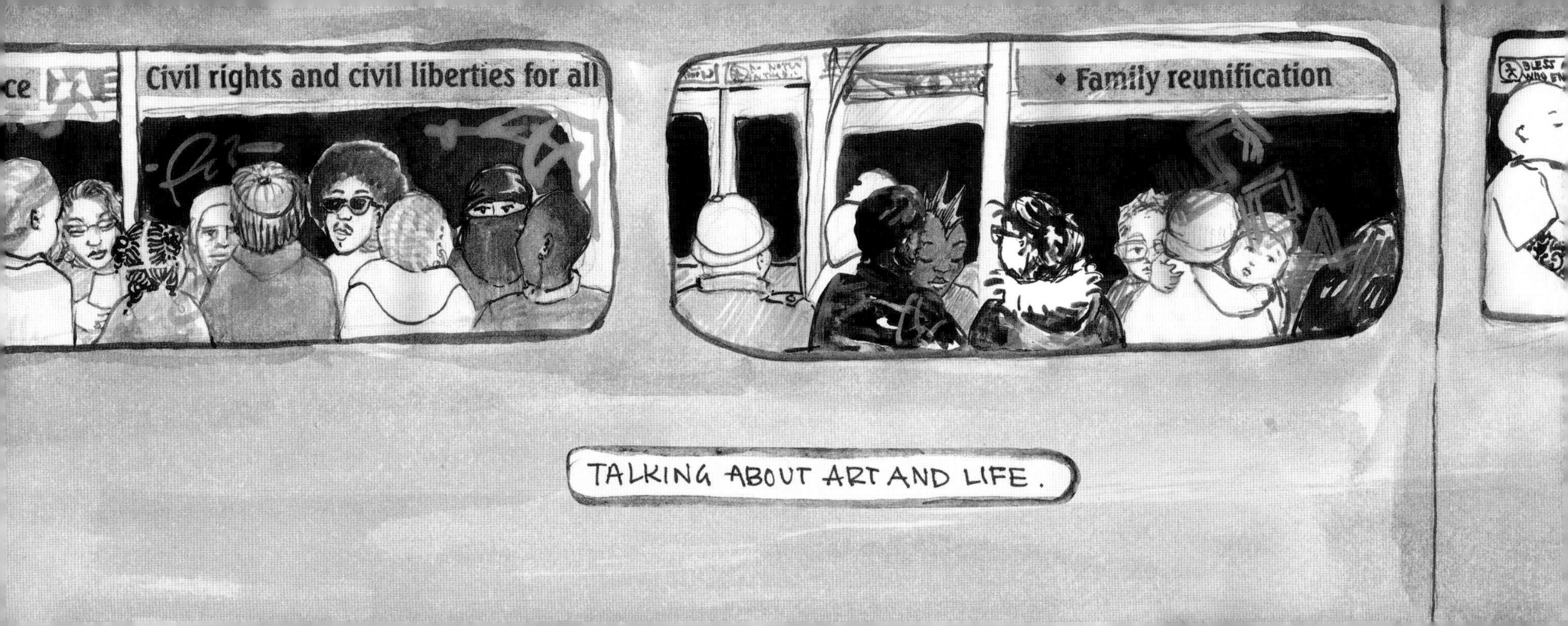
ce
Civil rights and civil liberties for all
Family reunification
TALKING ABOUT ART AND LIFE.

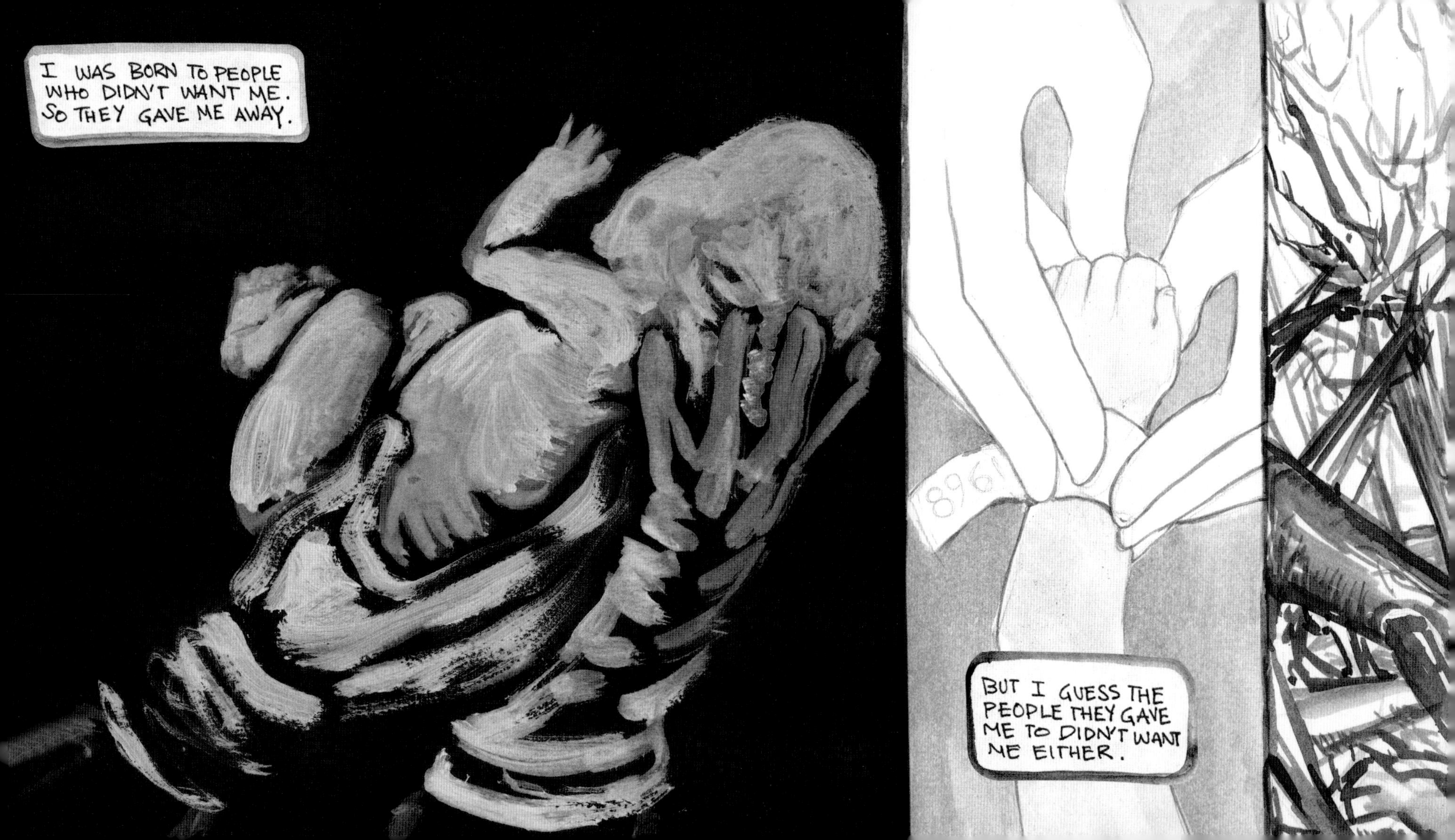
I WAS BORN TO PEOPLE WHO DIDN'T WANT ME. SO THEY GAVE ME AWAY.
BUT I GUESS THE PEOPLE THEY GAVE ME TO DIDN'T WANT ME EITHER.

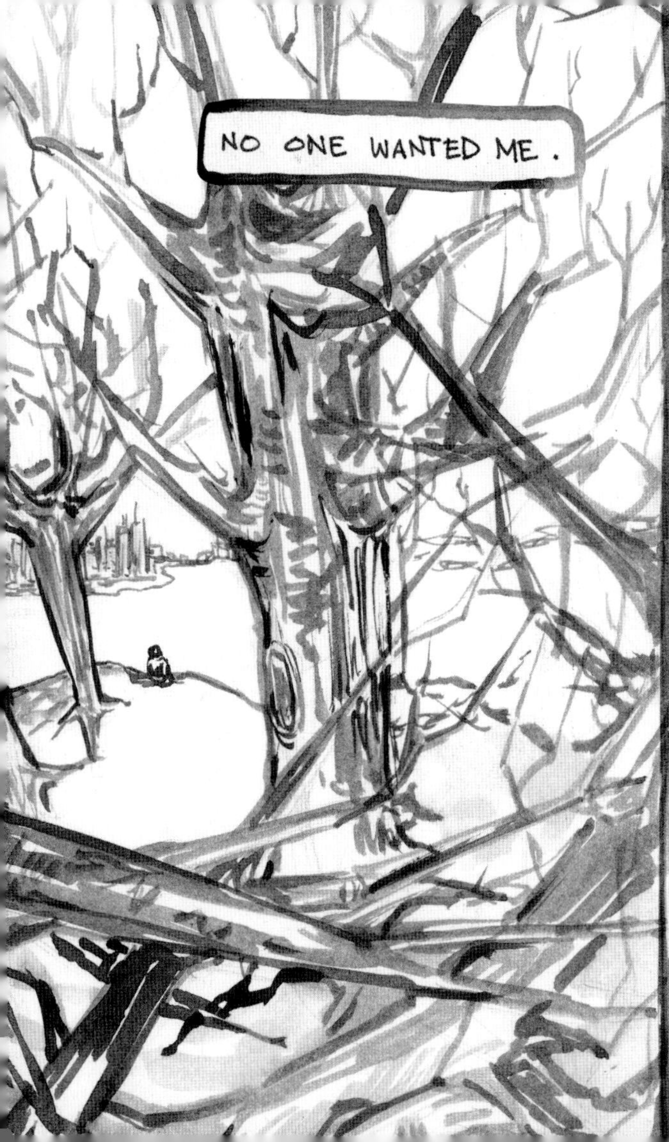
NO ONE WANTED ME.

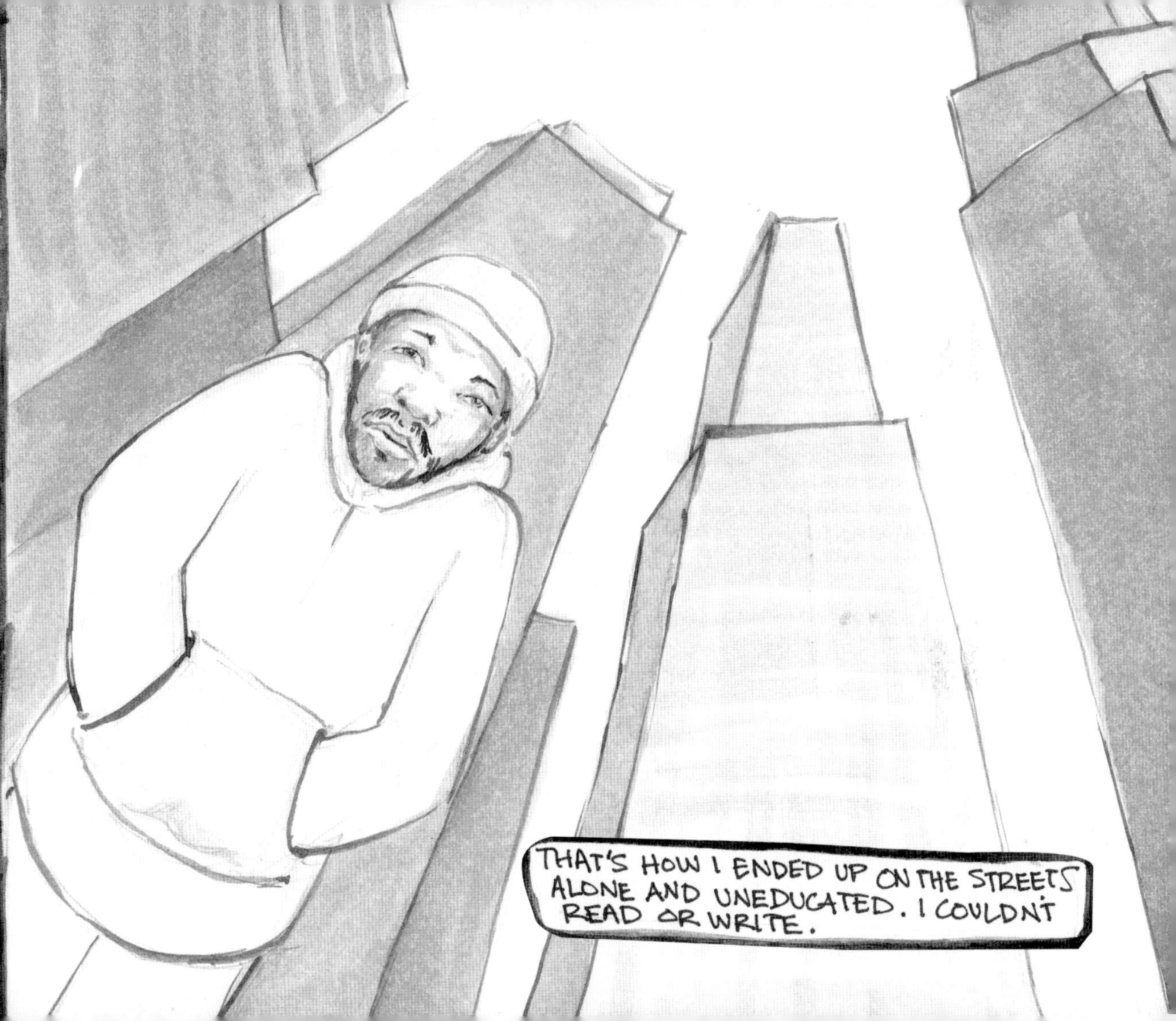
THAT'S HOW I ENDED UP ON THE STREETS ALONE AND UNEDUCATED. I COULDN'T READ OR WRITE.

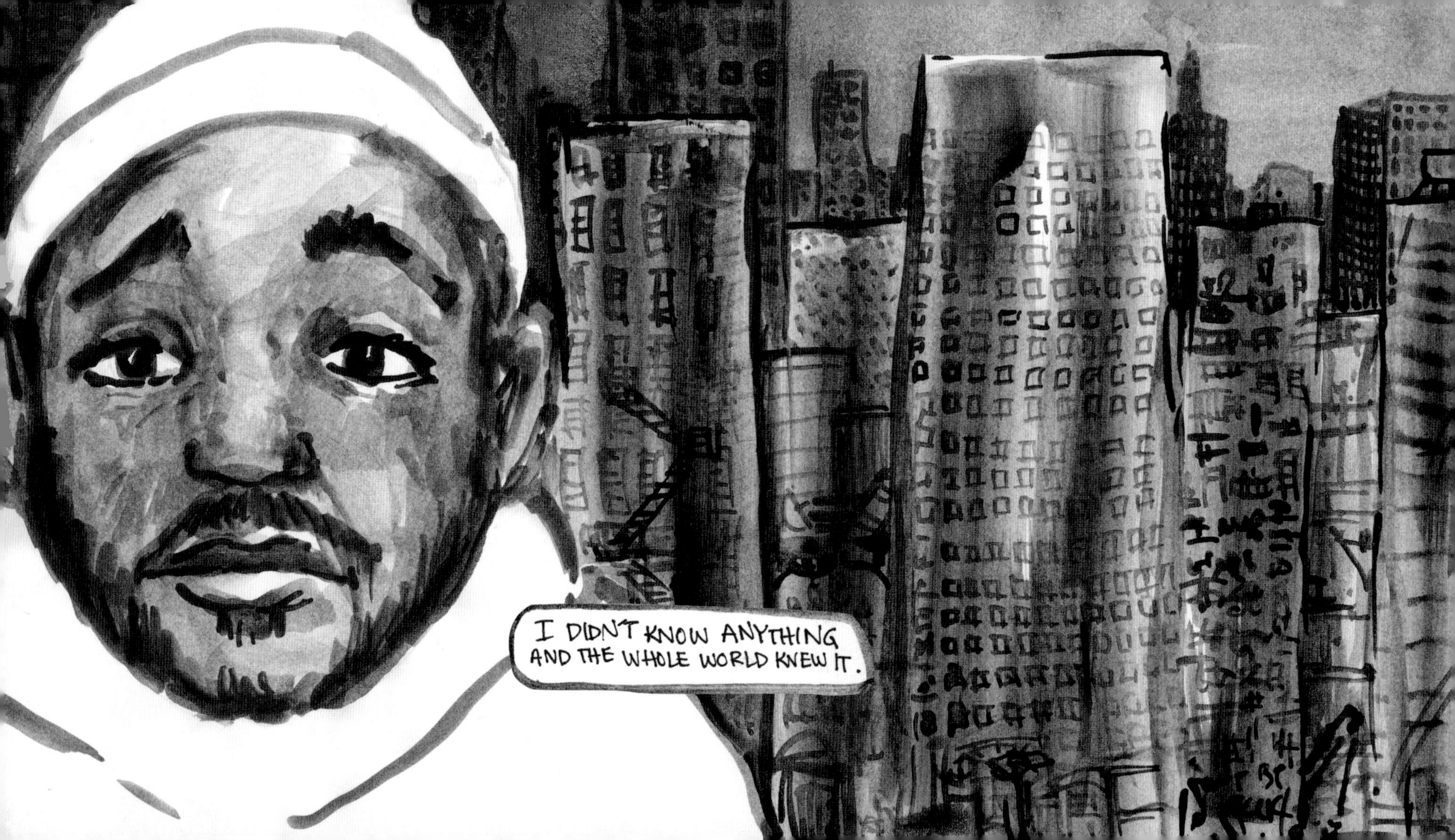
I DIDN'T KNOW ANYTHING AND THE WHOLE WORLD KNEW IT.

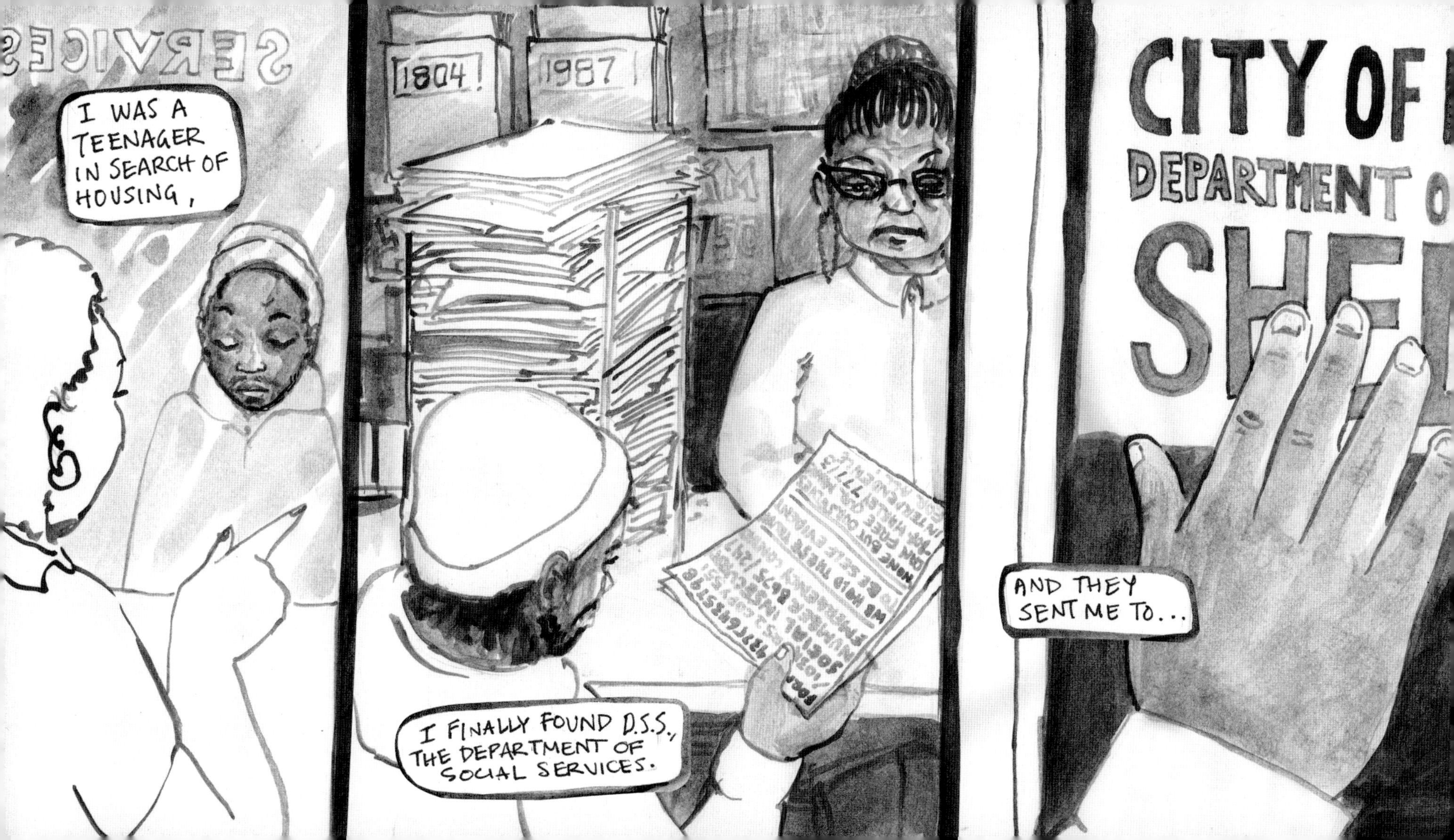
I WAS A TEENAGER IN SEARCH OF HOUSING,
1804
1987
I FINALLY FOUND D.S.S., THE DEPARTMENT OF SOCIAL SERVICES.
CITY OF
DEPARTMENT O
SHE
AND THEY SENT ME TO...

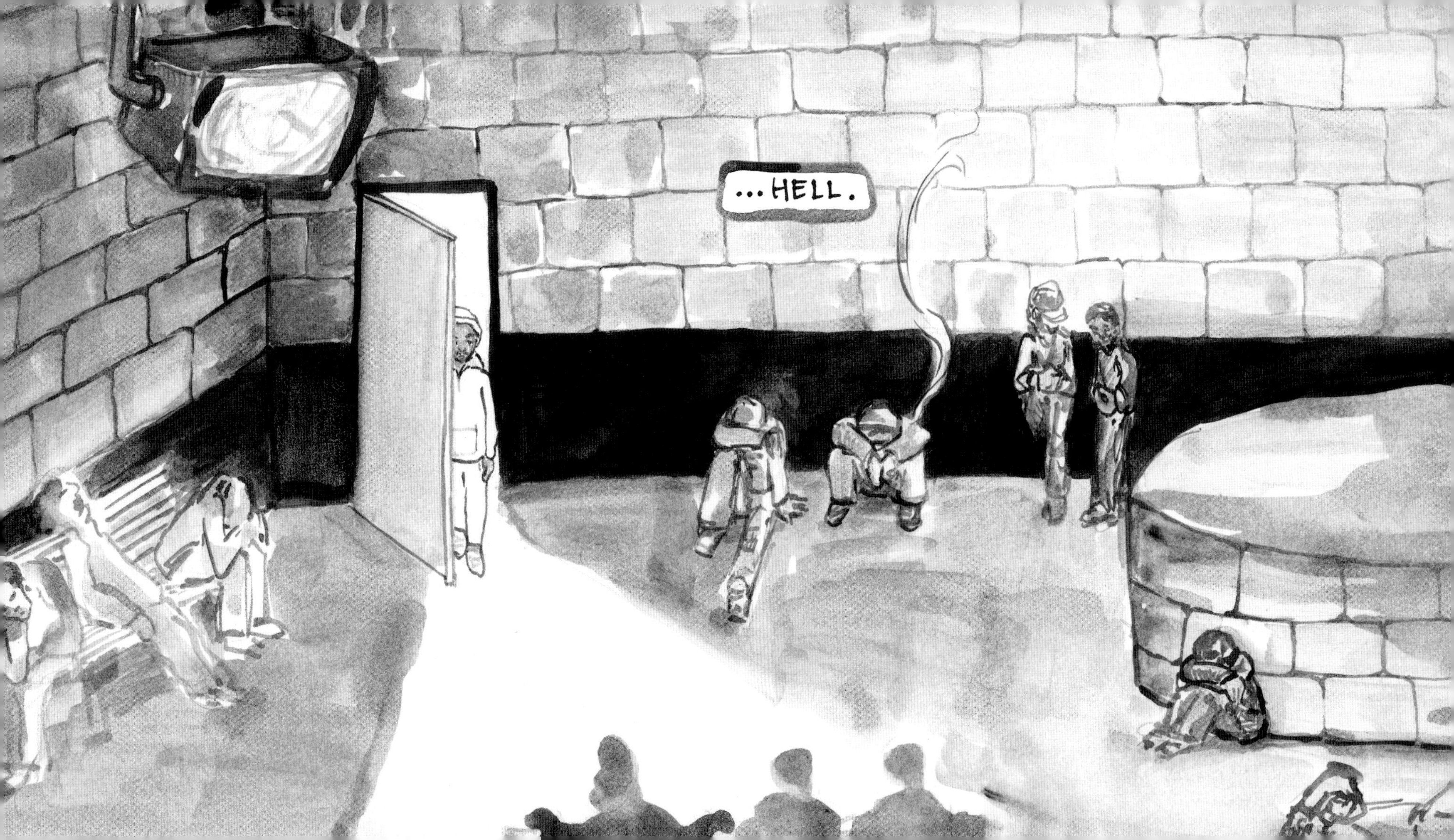
...HELL.

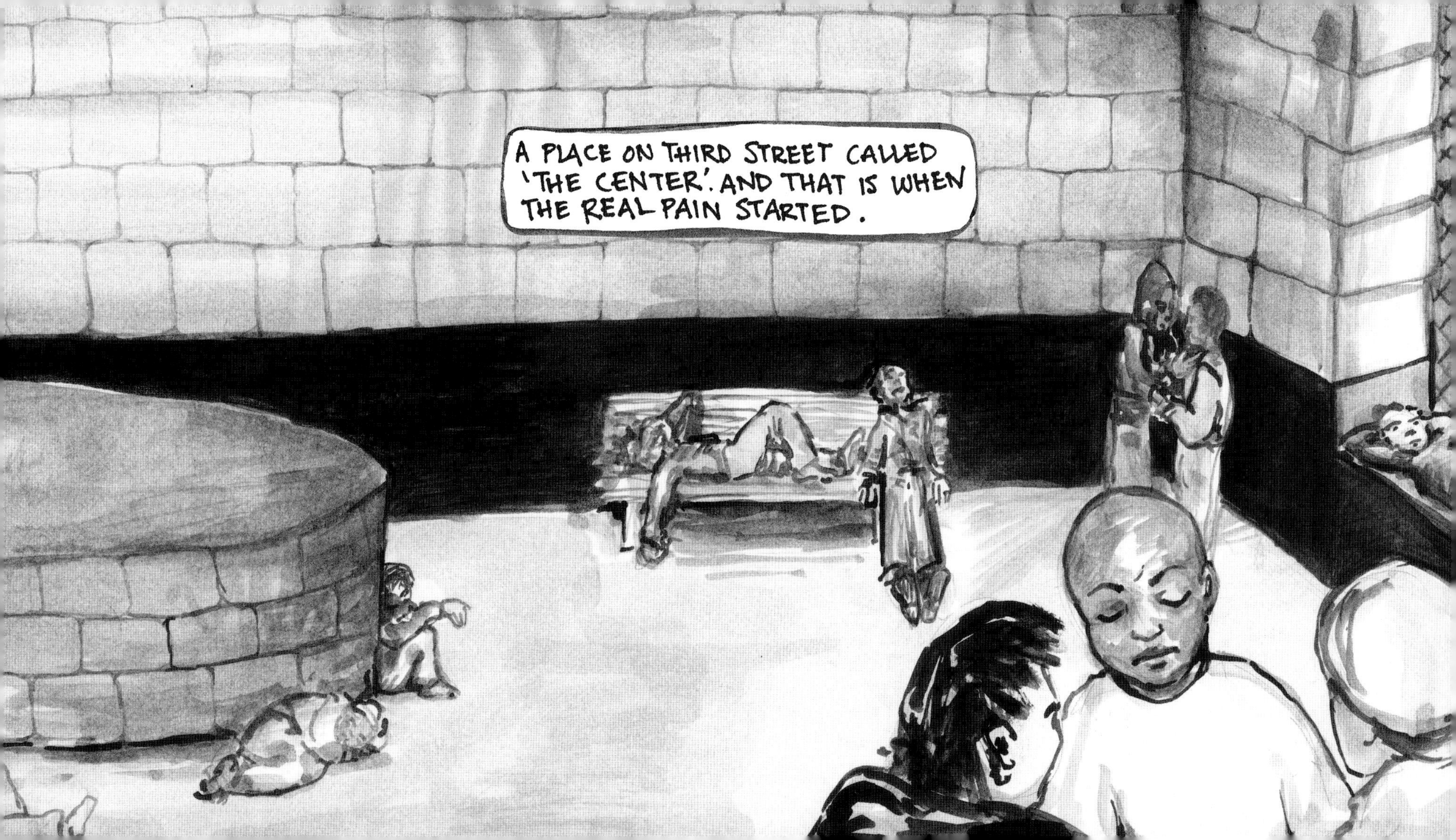
A PLACE ON THIRD STREET CALLED 'THE CENTER'. AND THAT IS WHEN THE REAL PAIN STARTED.

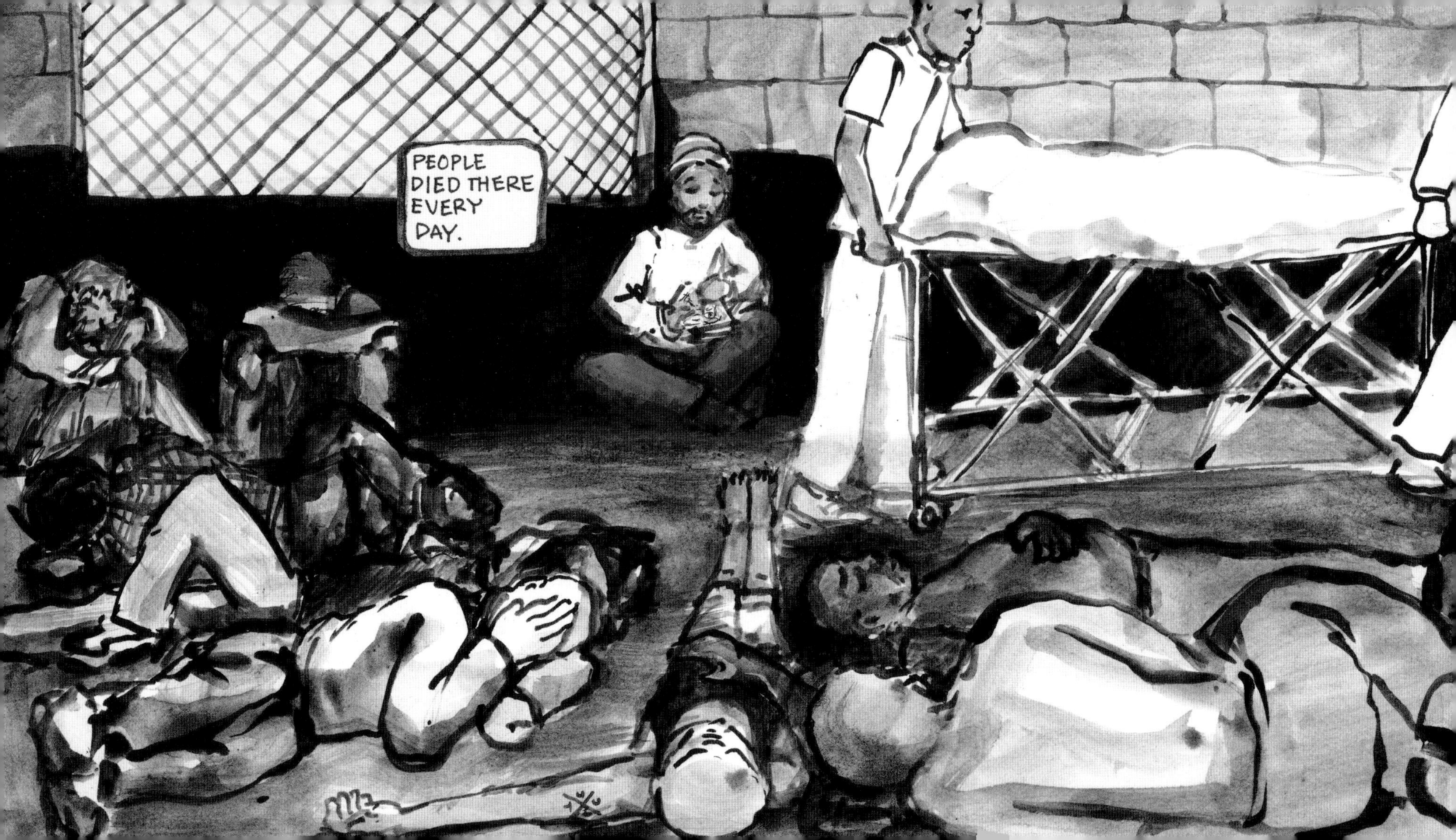
PEOPLE DIED THERE EVERY DAY.

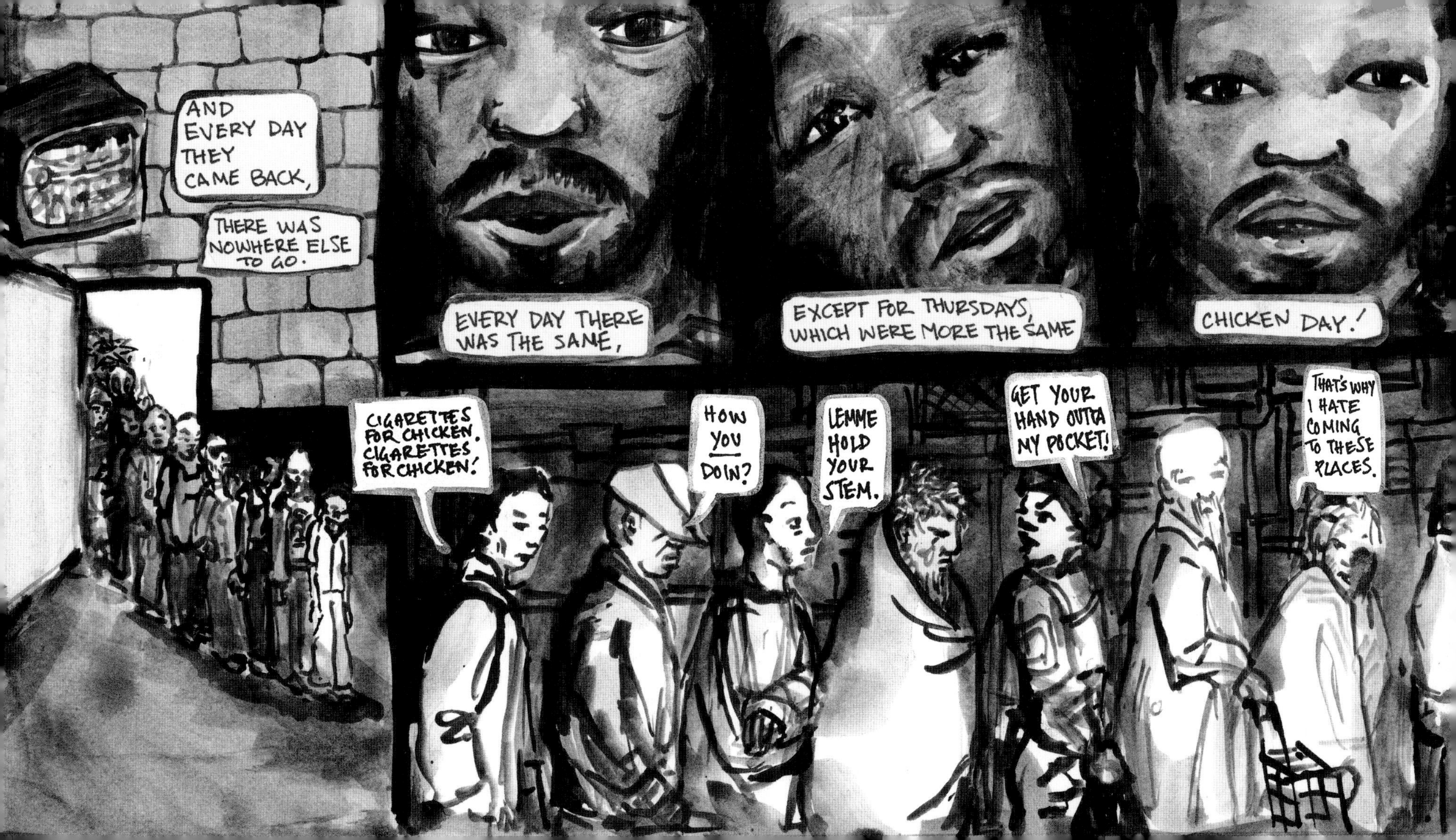

AND EVERY DAY THEY CAME BACK,
THERE WAS NOWHERE ELSE TO GO.
EVERY DAY THERE WAS THE SAME,
EXCEPT FOR THURSDAYS, WHICH WERE MORE THE SAME
CHICKEN DAY!
CIGARETTES FOR CHICKEN. CIGARETTES FOR CHICKEN!
HOW YOU DOIN?
LEMME HOLD YOUR STEM.
GET YOUR HAND OUTTA MY POCKET!
THAT'S WHY I HATE COMING TO THESE PLACES.

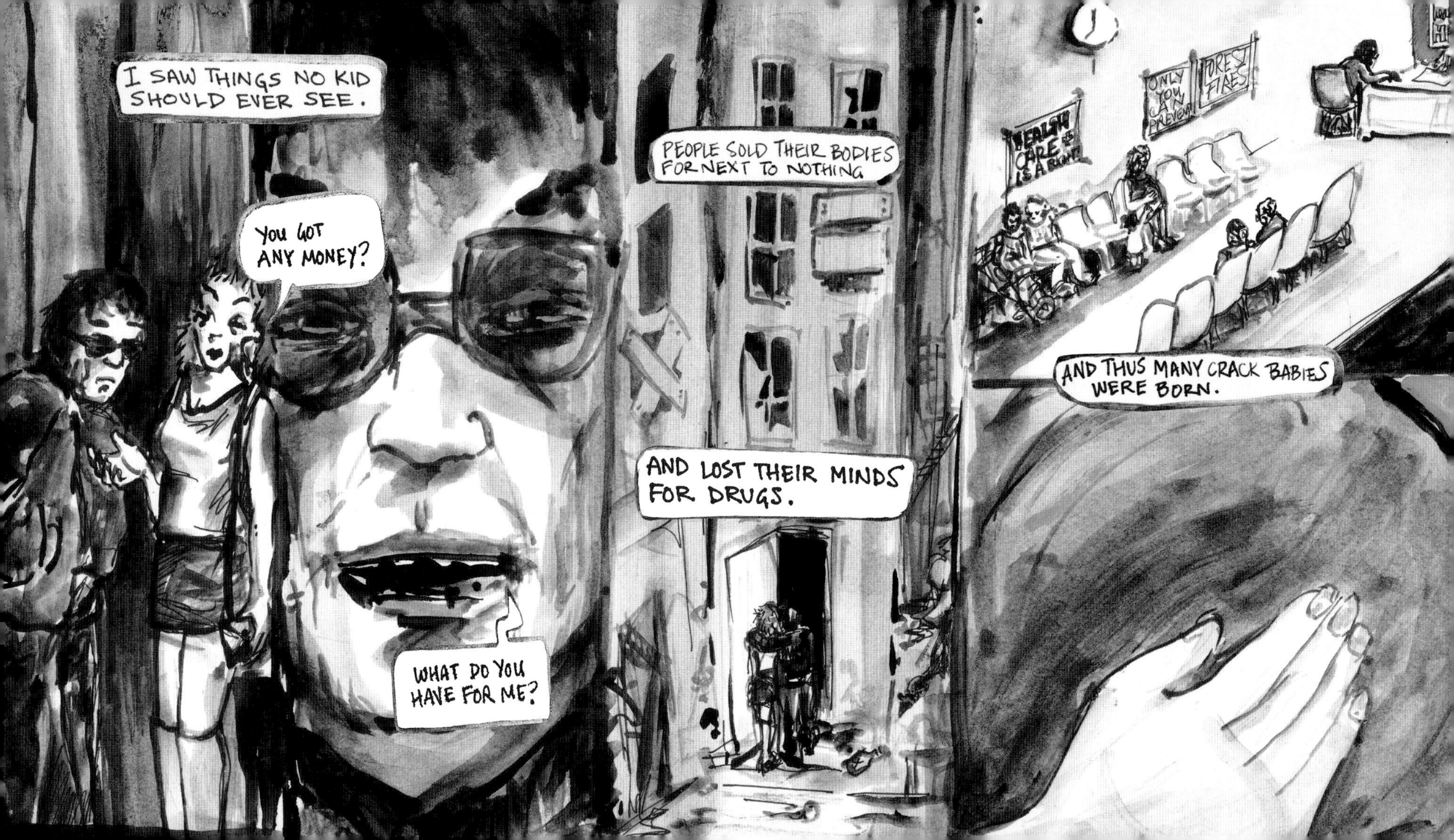
I SAW THINGS NO KID SHOULD EVER SEE.
YOU GOT ANY MONEY?
WHAT DO YOU HAVE FOR ME?
PEOPLE SOLD THEIR BODIES FOR NEXT TO NOTHING
AND LOST THEIR MINDS FOR DRUGS.
HEALTH CARE IS A RIGHT!
ONLY YOU CAN PREVENT
FOREST FIRES
AND THUS MANY CRACK BABIES WERE BORN.

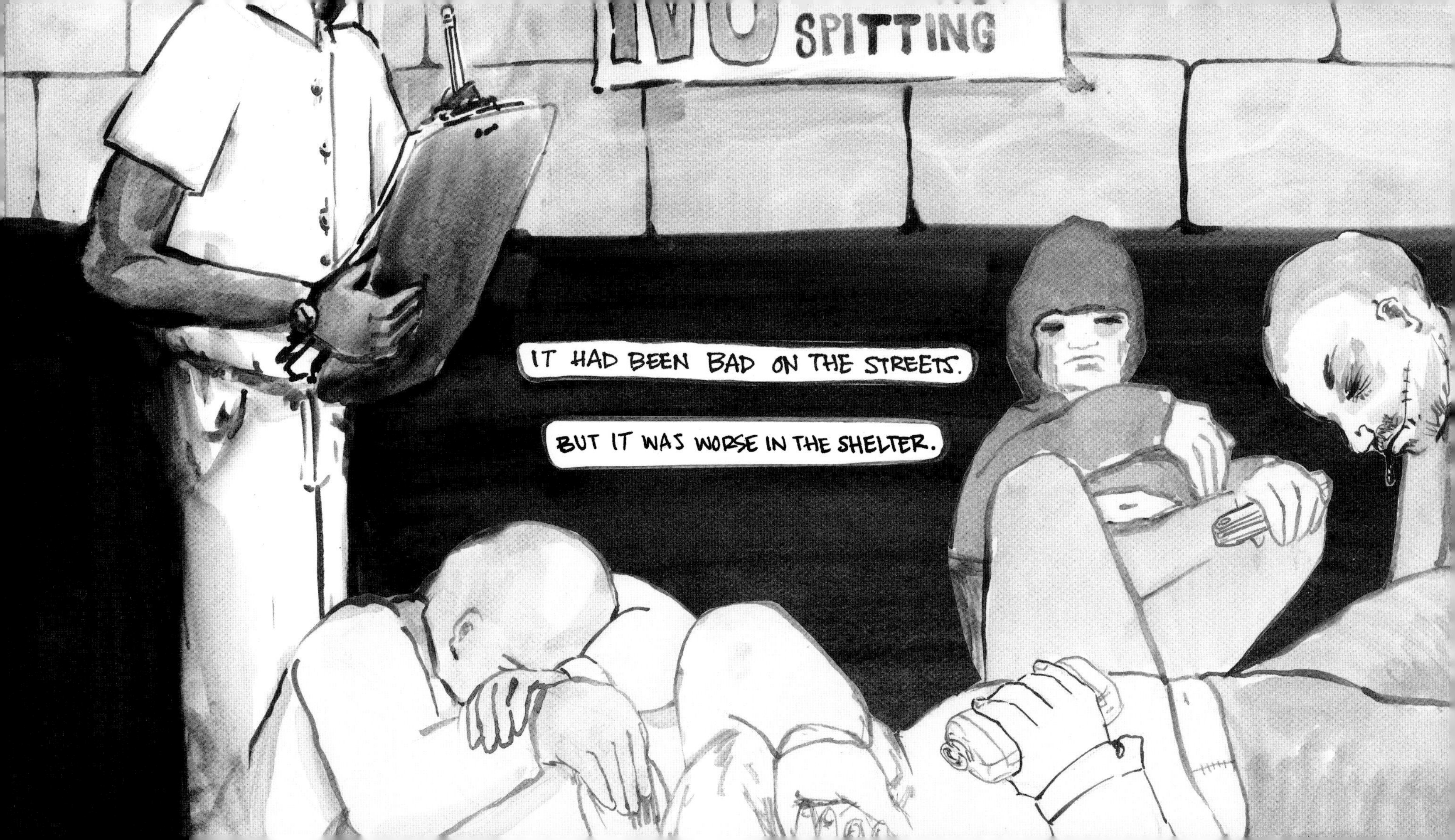
SPITTING
IT HAD BEEN BAD ON THE STREETS.
BUT IT WAS WORSE IN THE SHELTER.

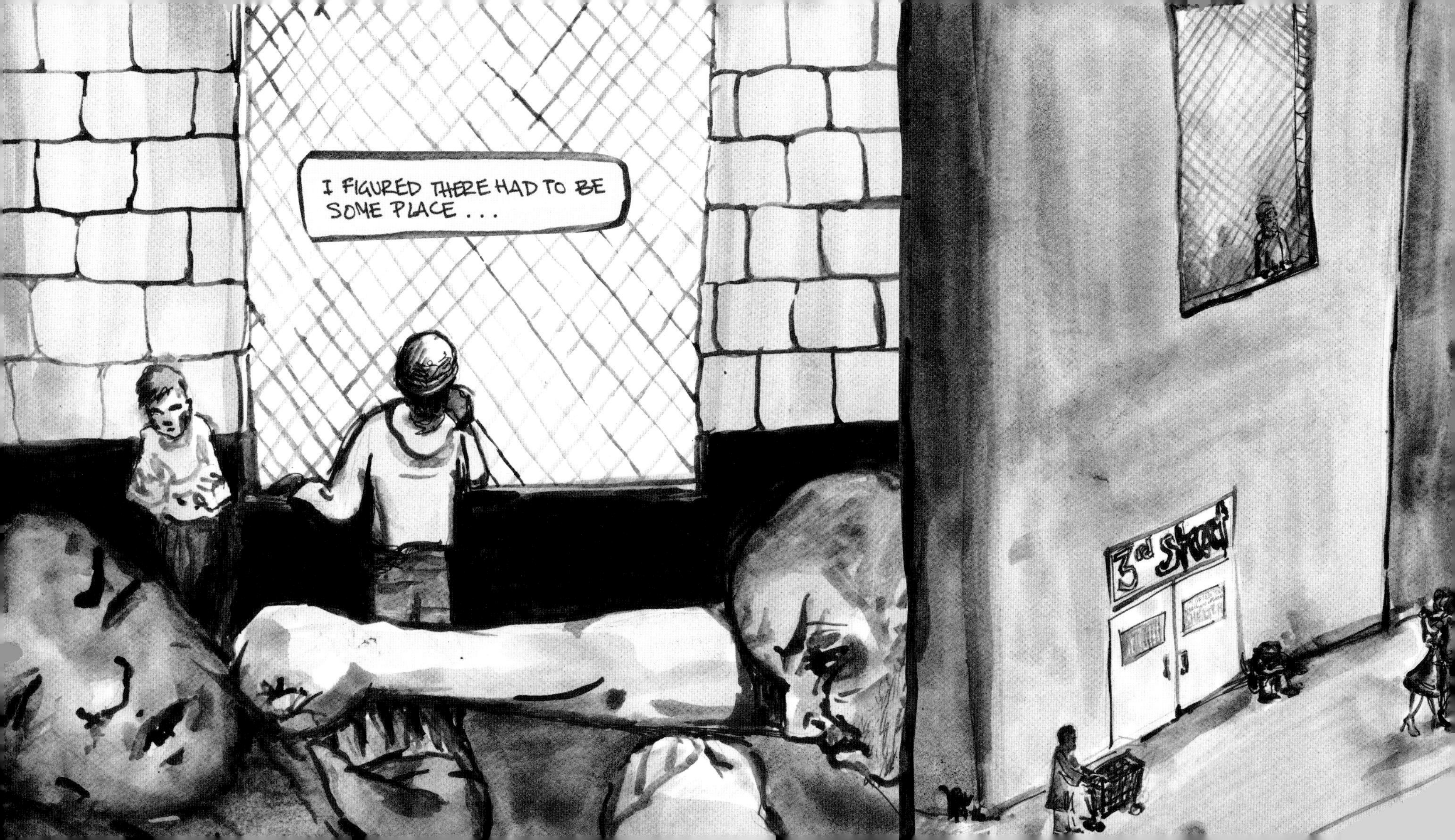
I FIGURED THERE HAD TO BE SOME PLACE . . .

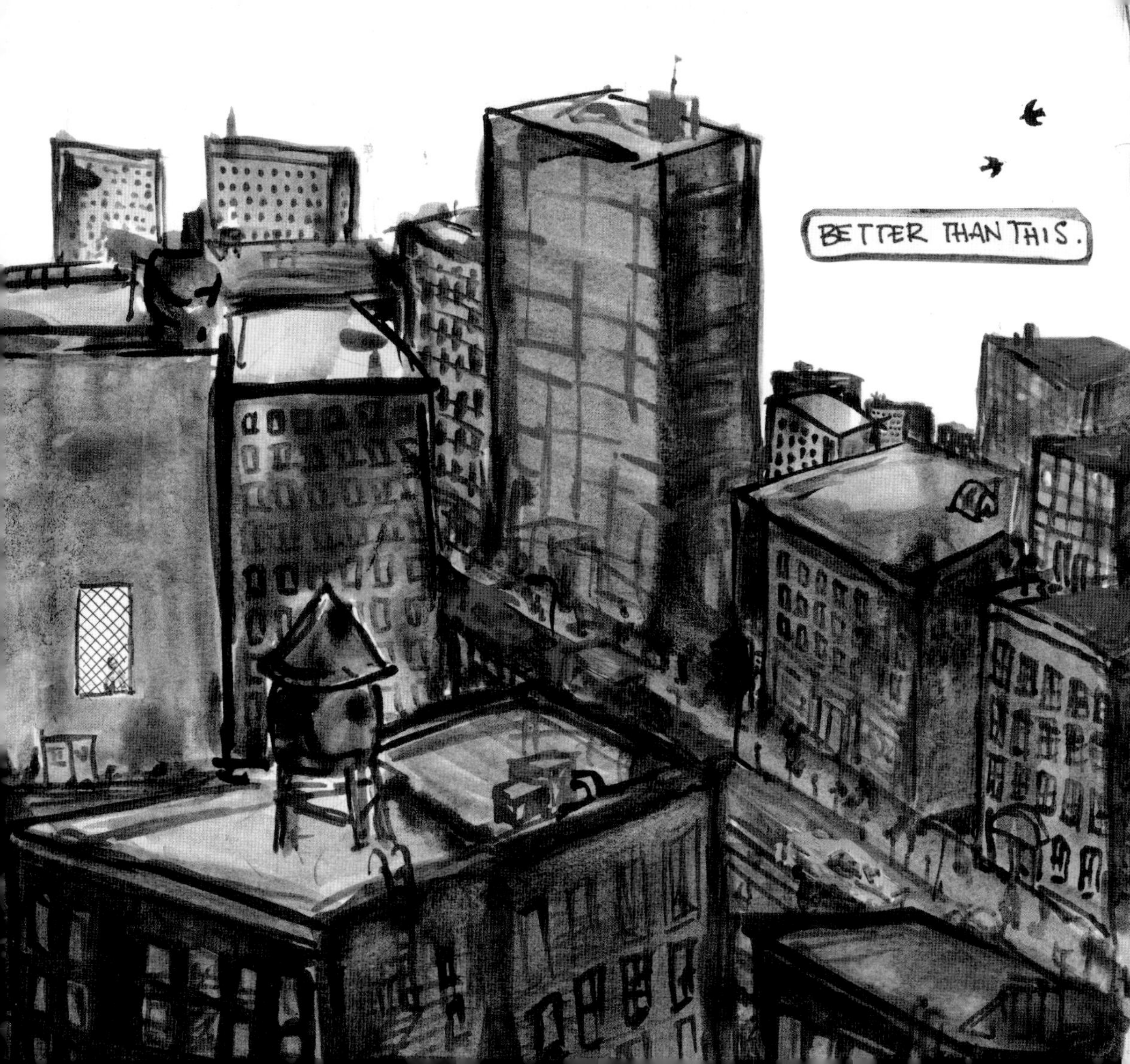
BETTER THAN THIS.

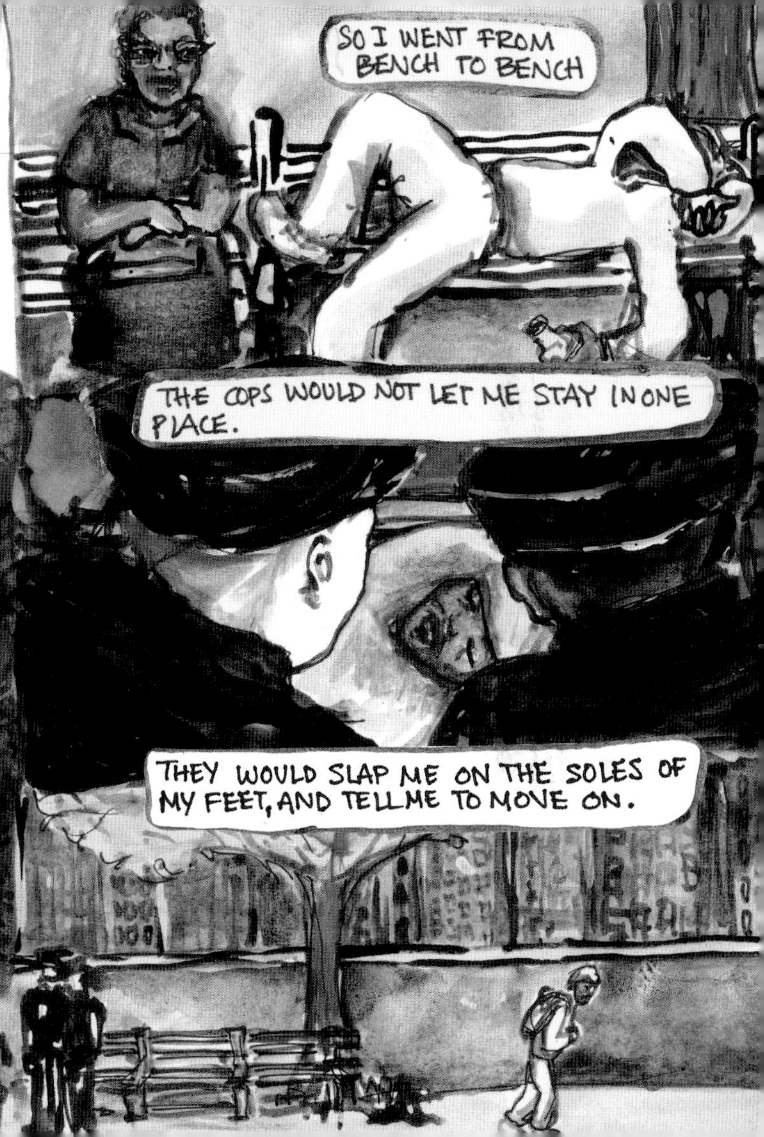
SO I WENT FROM BENCH TO BENCH
THE COPS WOULD NOT LET ME STAY IN ONE PLACE.
THEY WOULD SLAP ME ON THE SOLES OF MY FEET, AND TELL ME TO MOVE ON.

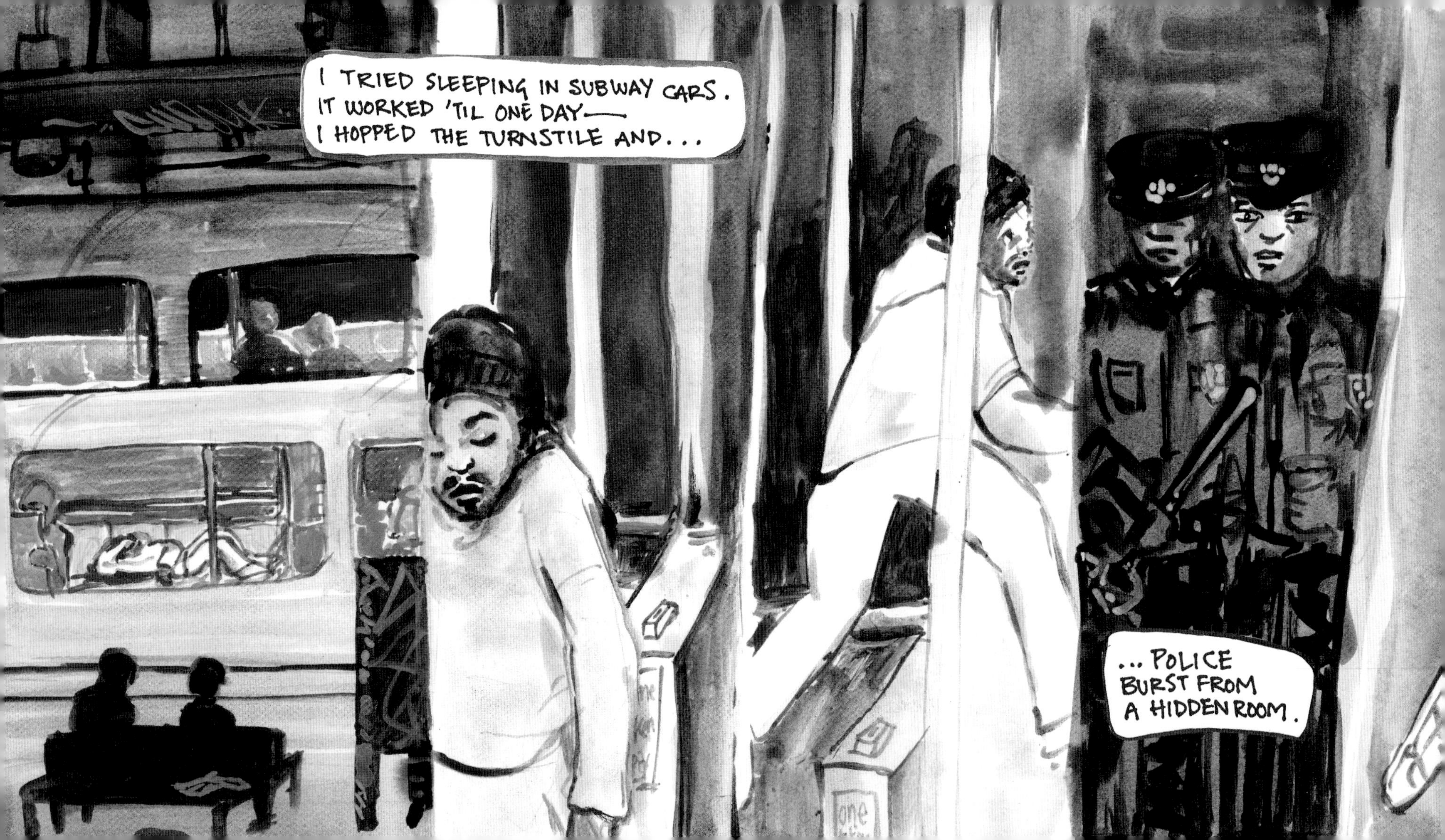
I TRIED SLEEPING IN SUBWAY CARS. IT WORKED 'TIL ONE DAY— I HOPPED THE TURNSTILE AND...
...POLICE BURST FROM A HIDDEN ROOM.

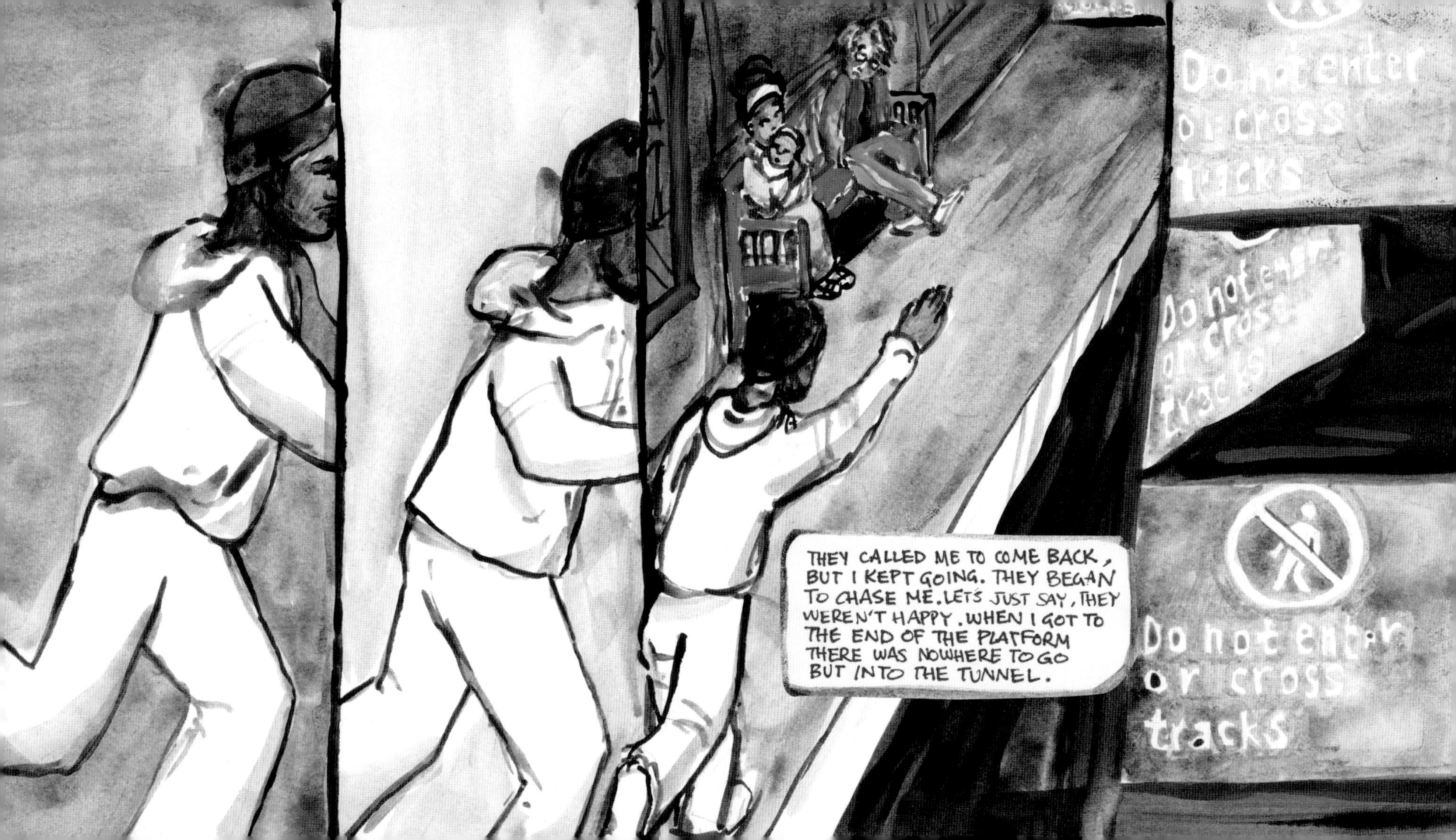
THEY CALLED ME TO COME BACK, BUT I KEPT GOING. THEY BEGAN TO CHASE ME. LET'S JUST SAY, THEY WEREN'T HAPPY. WHEN I GOT TO THE END OF THE PLATFORM THERE WAS NOWHERE TO GO BUT INTO THE TUNNEL.
Do not enter or cross tracks

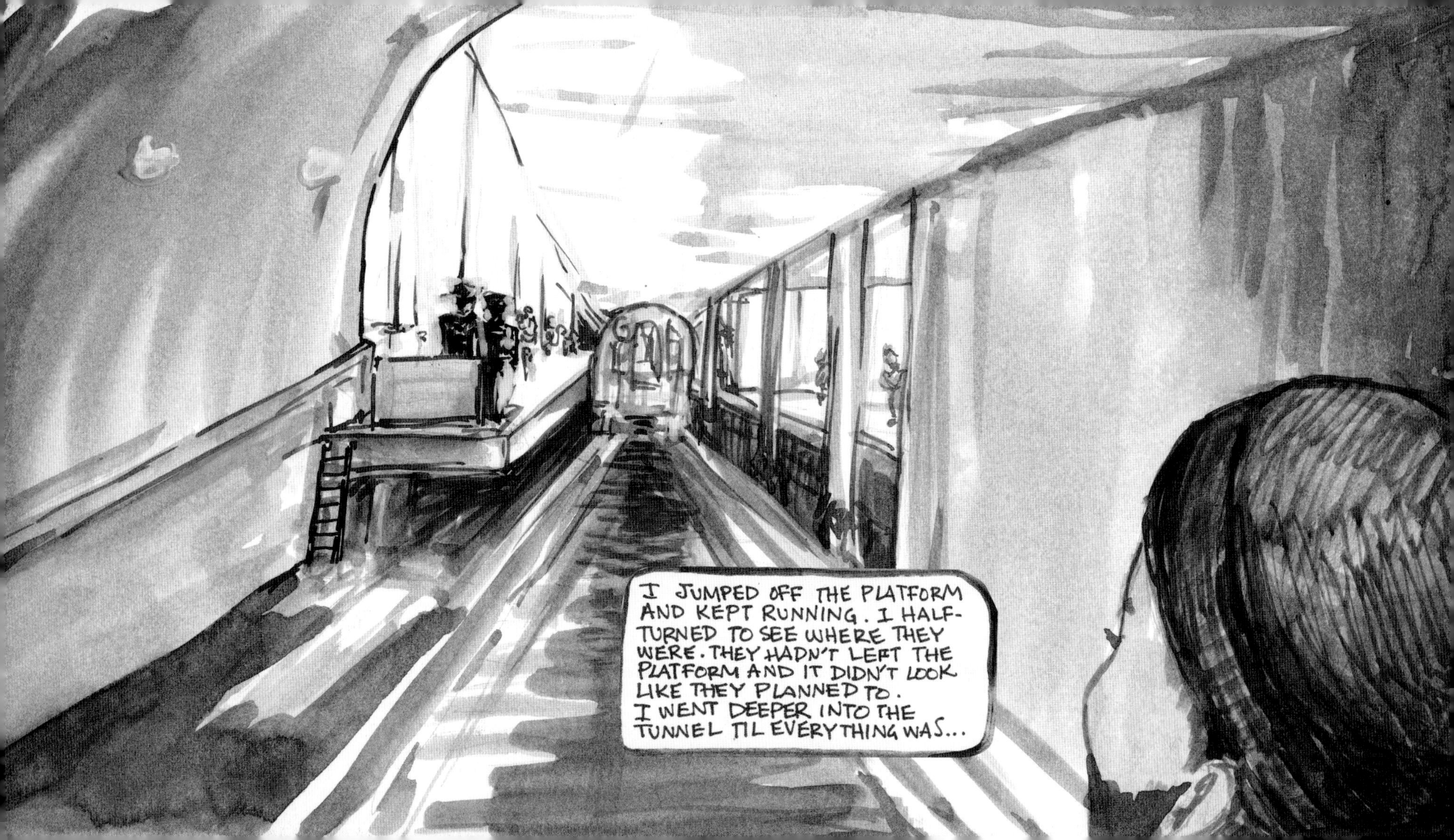
I JUMPED OFF THE PLATFORM AND KEPT RUNNING. I HALF-TURNED TO SEE WHERE THEY WERE. THEY HADN'T LEFT THE PLATFORM AND IT DIDN'T LOOK LIKE THEY PLANNED TO. I WENT DEEPER INTO THE TUNNEL TIL EVERYTHING WAS...

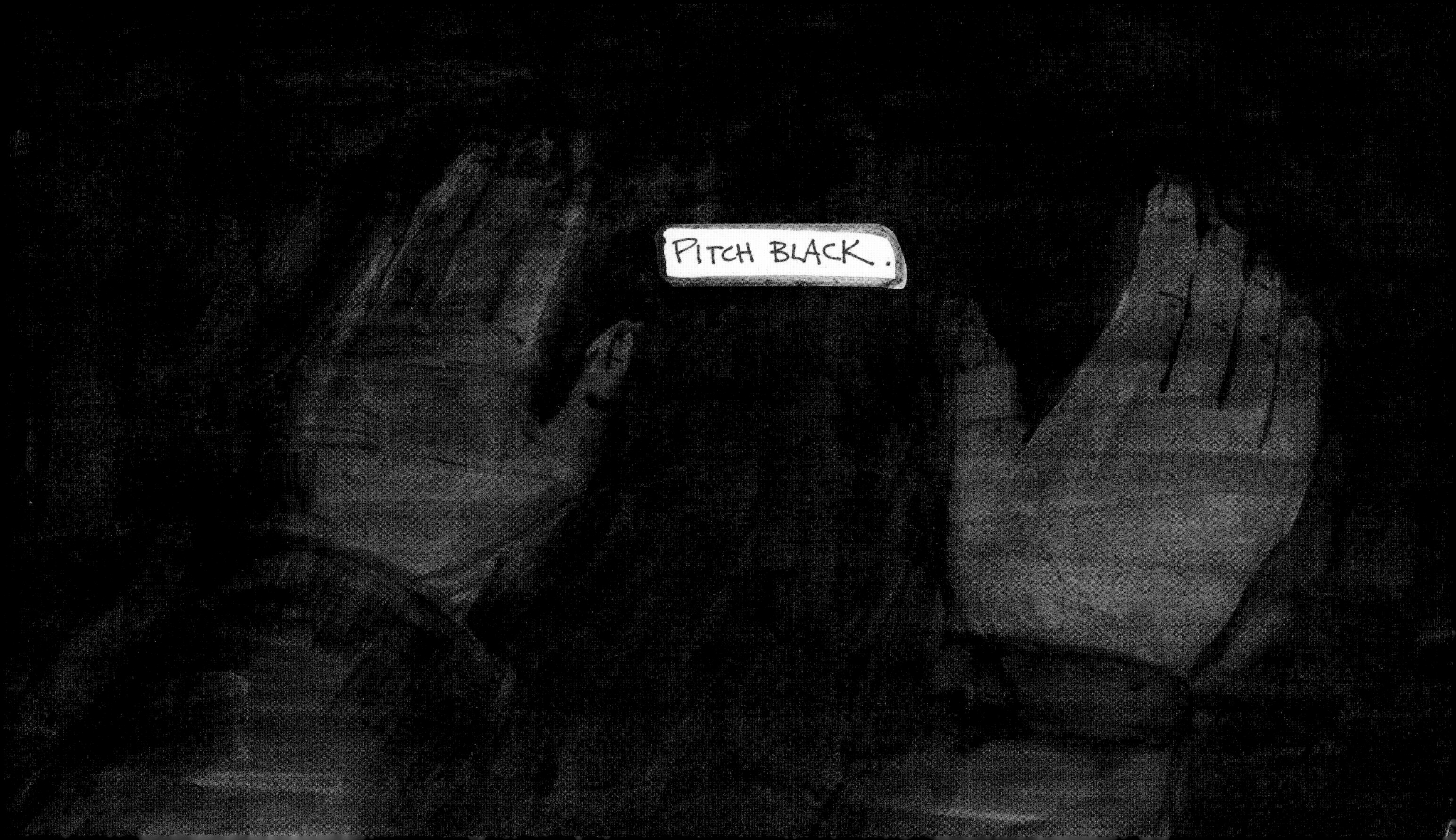
PITCH BLACK.

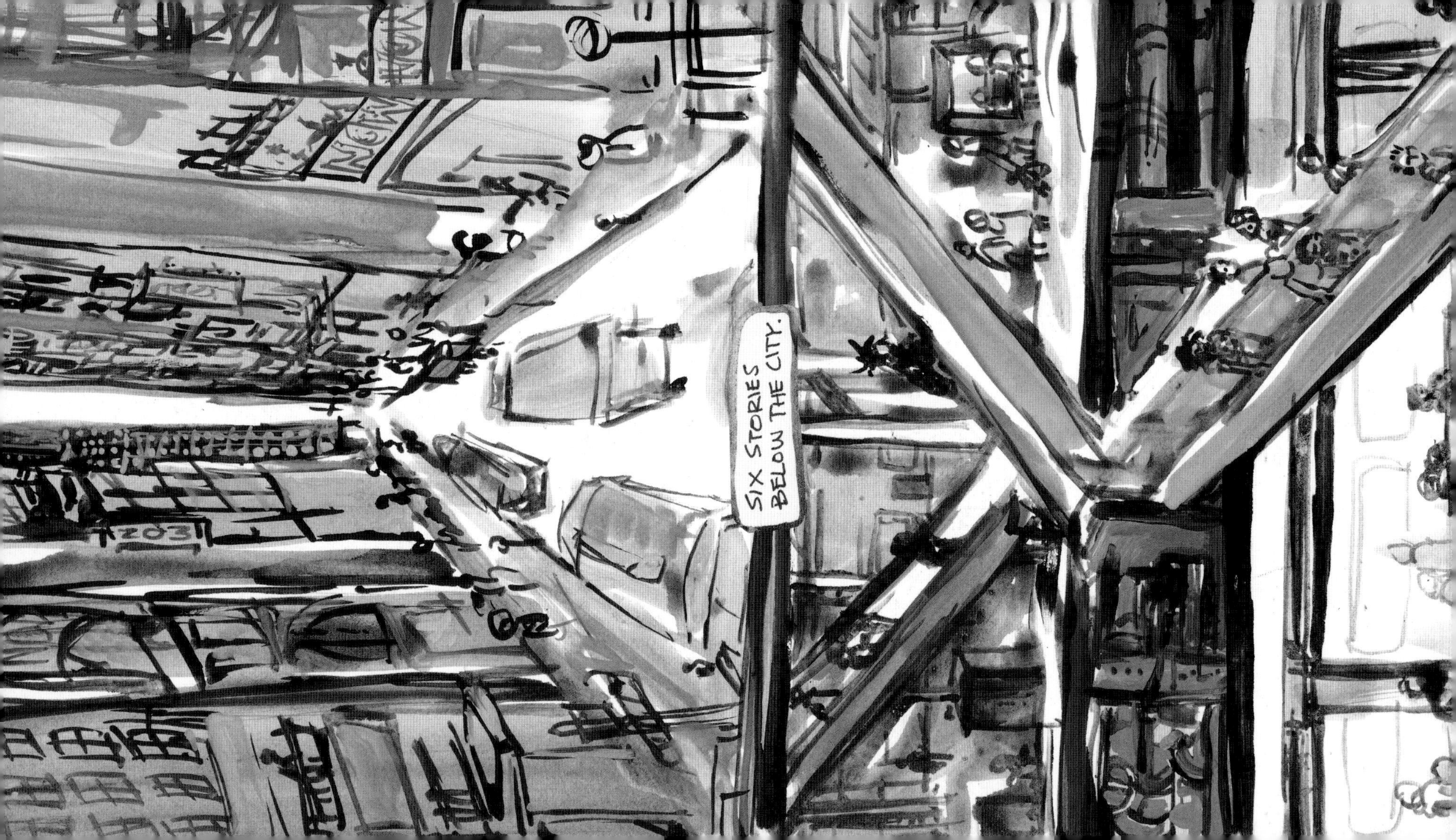
SIX STORIES BELOW THE CITY.
203

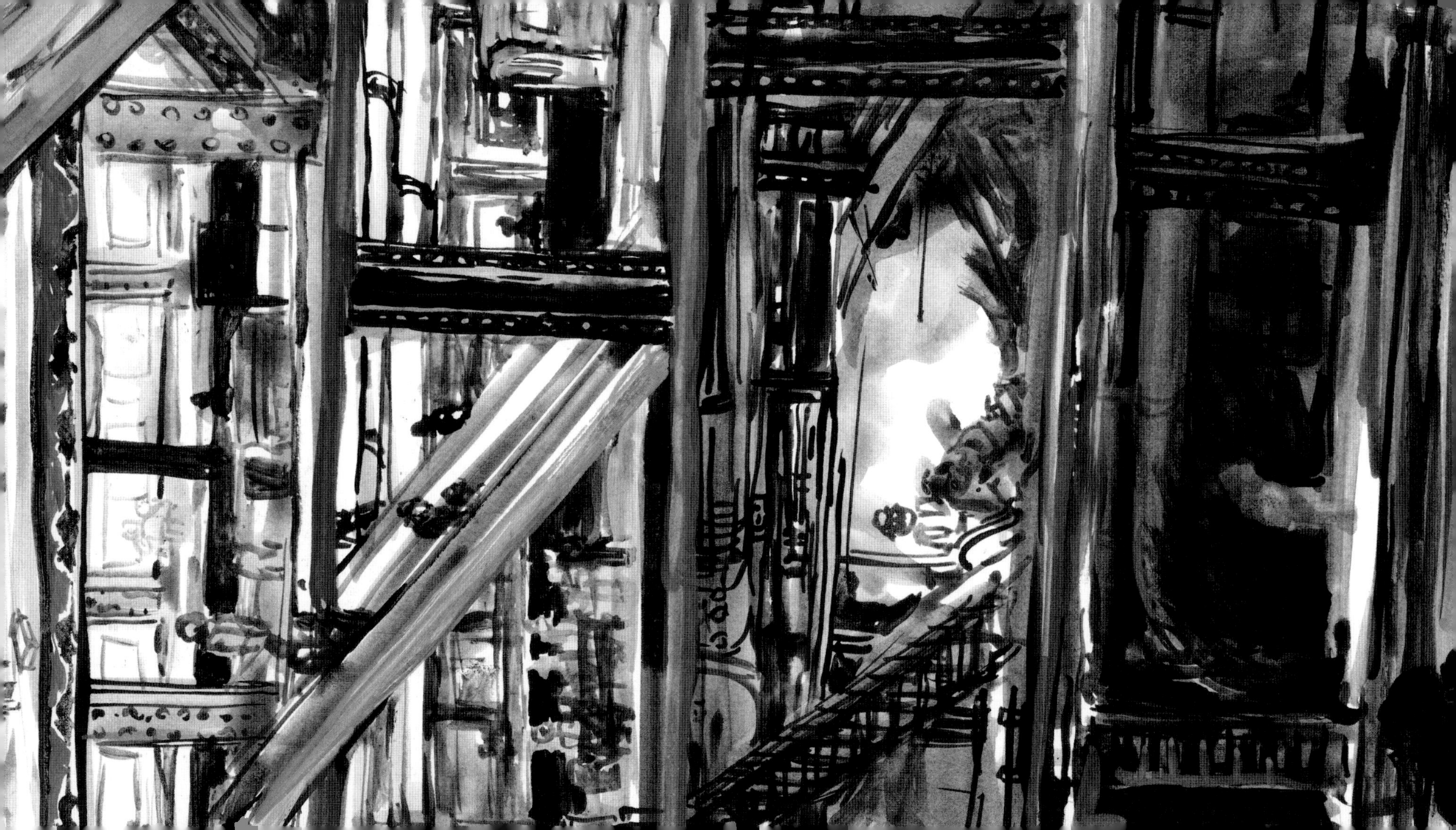

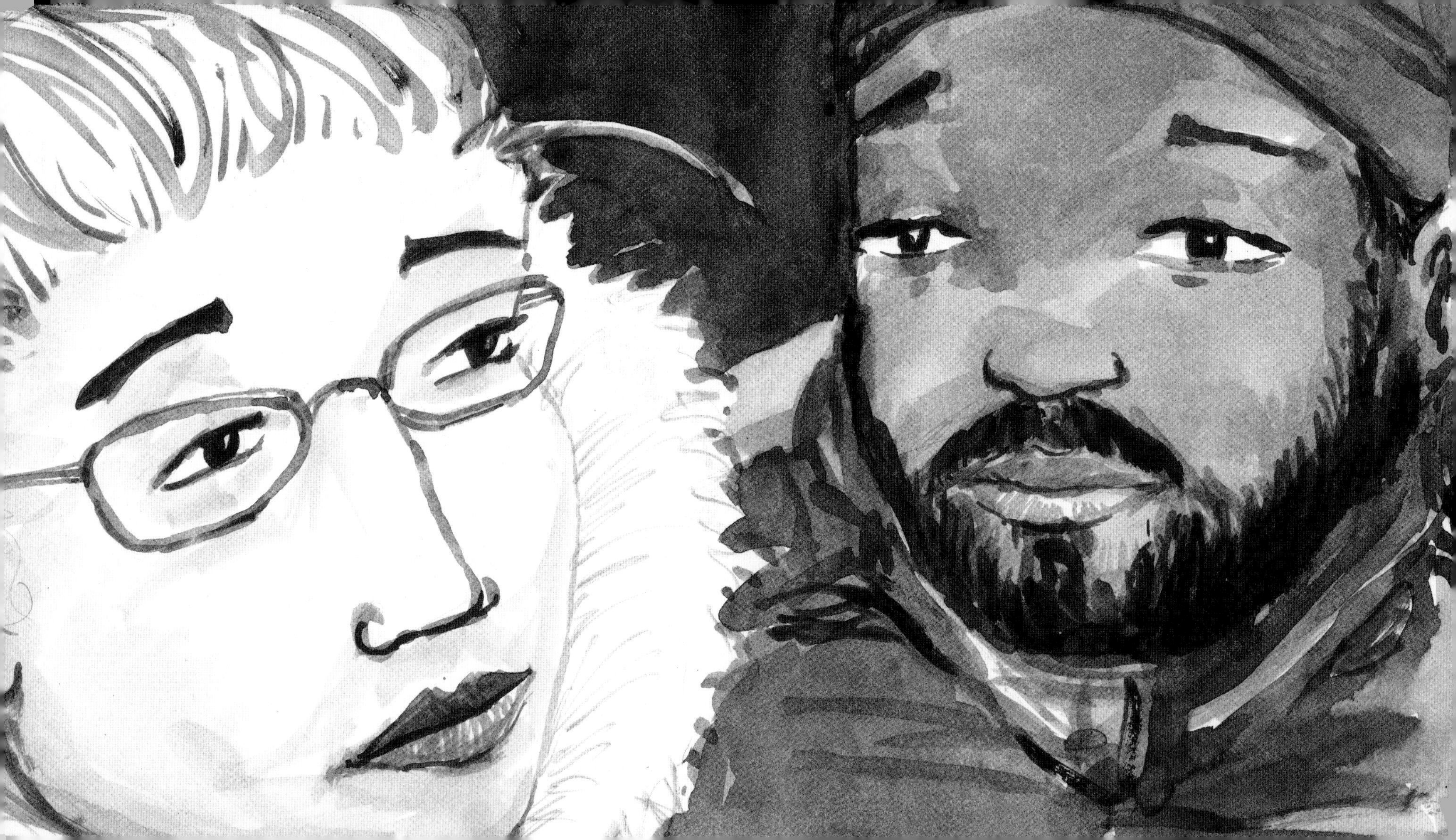

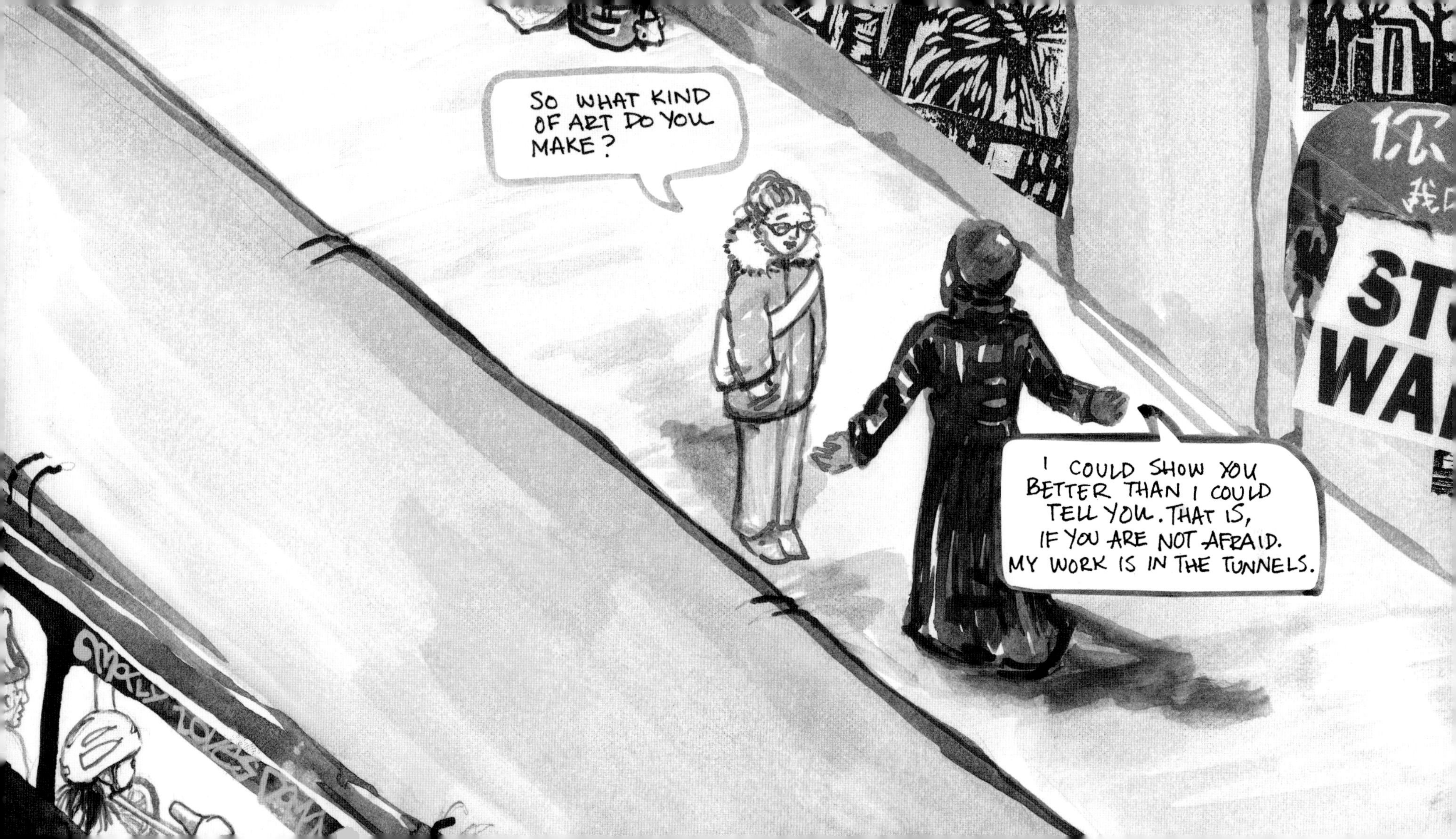
SO WHAT KIND OF ART DO YOU MAKE?
I COULD SHOW YOU BETTER THAN I COULD TELL YOU. THAT IS, IF YOU ARE NOT AFRAID. MY WORK IS IN THE TUNNELS.

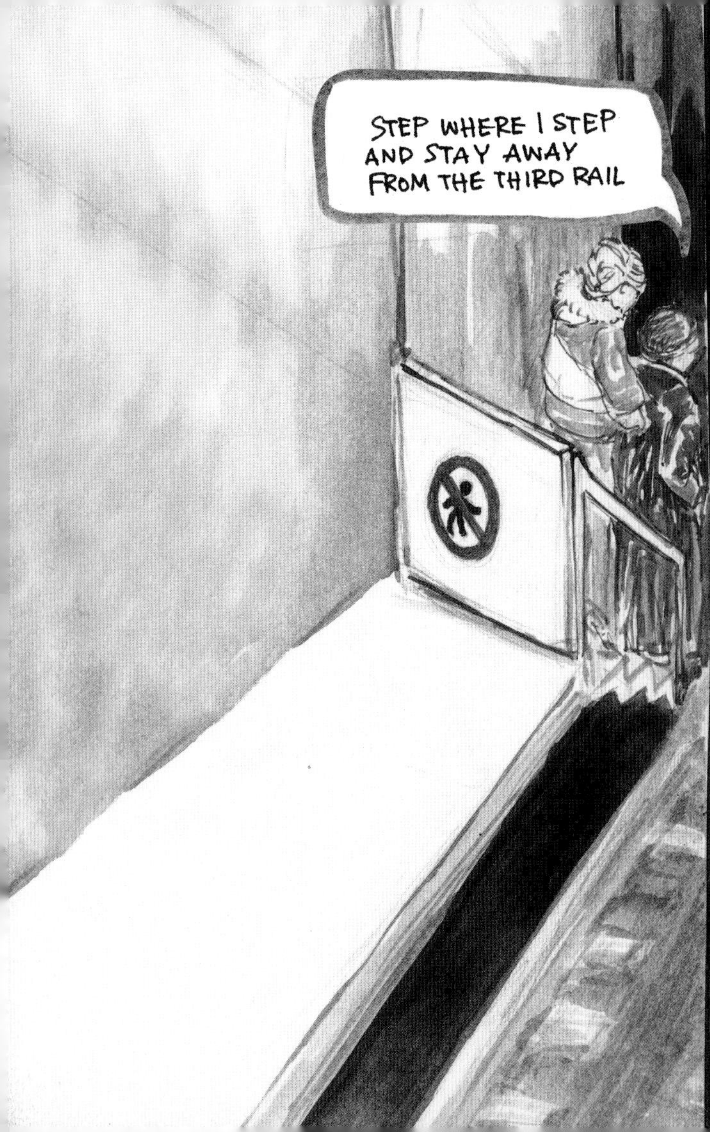
STEP WHERE I STEP AND STAY AWAY FROM THE THIRD RAIL

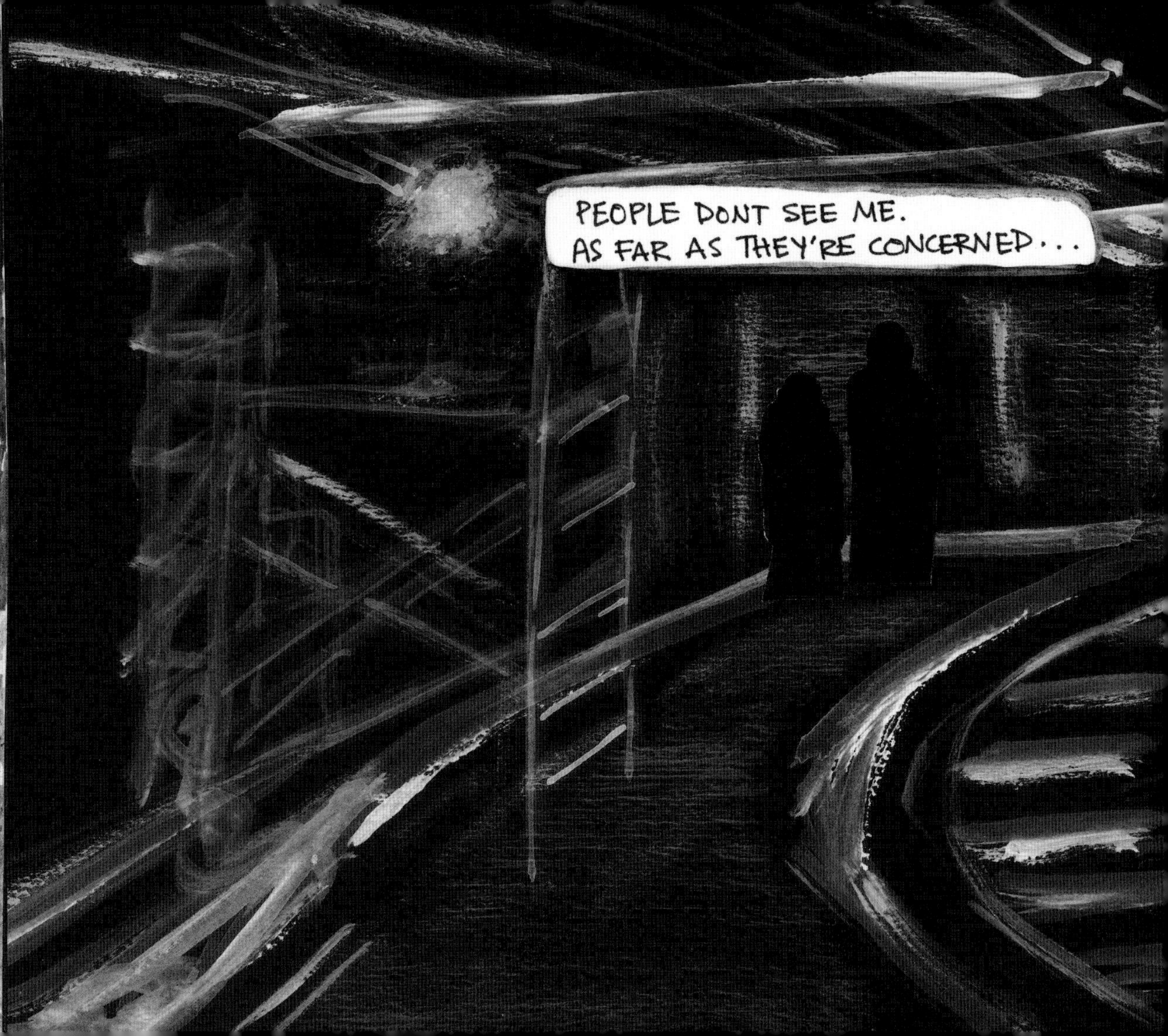
PEOPLE DONT SEE ME. AS FAR AS THEY'RE CONCERNED...

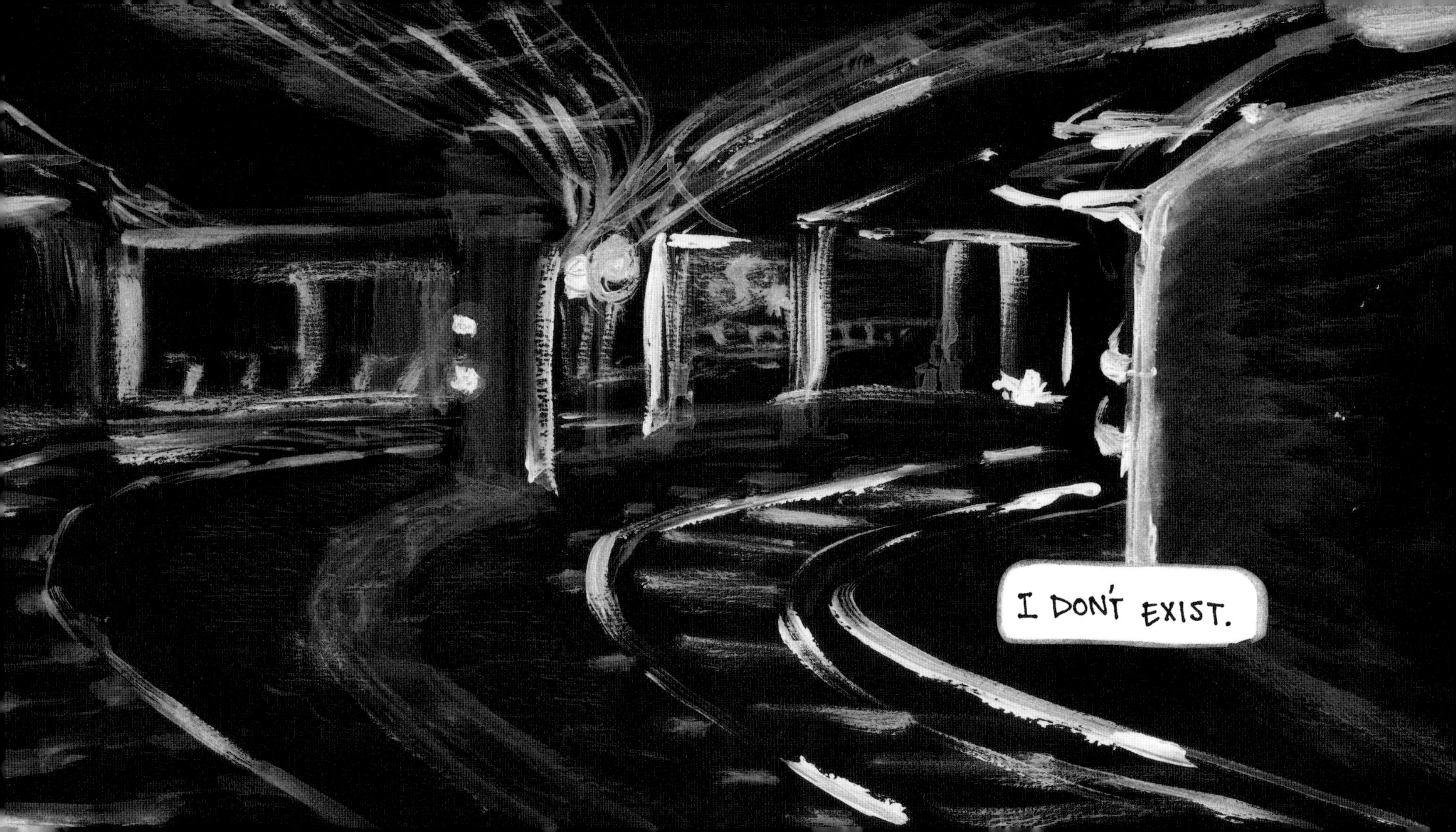
I DON'T EXIST.

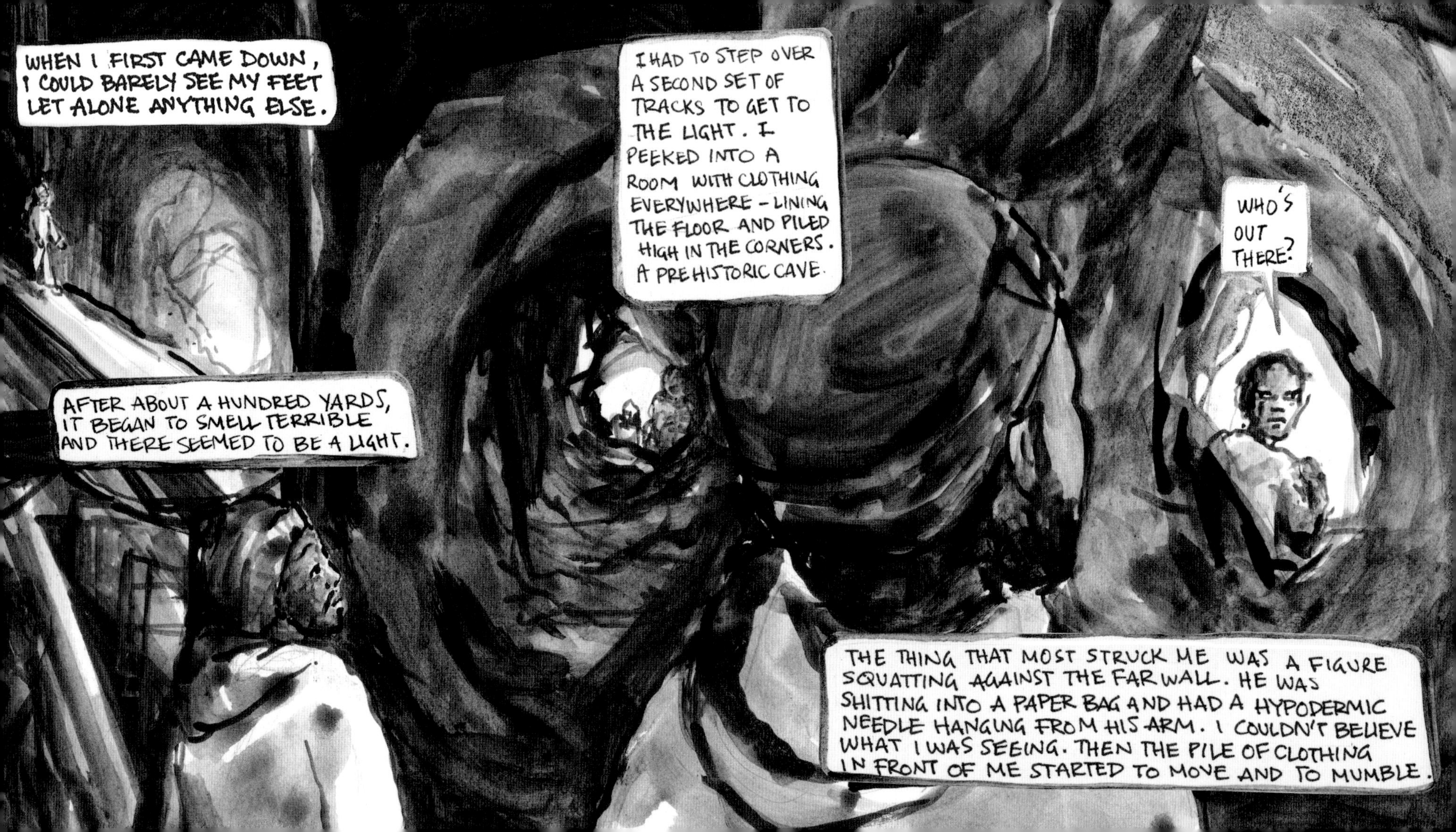
WHEN I FIRST CAME DOWN, I COULD BARELY SEE MY FEET LET ALONE ANYTHING ELSE.
AFTER ABOUT A HUNDRED YARDS, IT BEGAN TO SMELL TERRIBLE AND THERE SEEMED TO BE A LIGHT.
I HAD TO STEP OVER A SECOND SET OF TRACKS TO GET TO THE LIGHT. I PEEKED INTO A ROOM WITH CLOTHING EVERYWHERE – LINING THE FLOOR AND PILED HIGH IN THE CORNERS. A PREHISTORIC CAVE.
WHO'S OUT THERE?
THE THING THAT MOST STRUCK ME WAS A FIGURE SQUATTING AGAINST THE FAR WALL. HE WAS SHITTING INTO A PAPER BAG AND HAD A HYPODERMIC NEEDLE HANGING FROM HIS ARM. I COULDN'T BELIEVE WHAT I WAS SEEING. THEN THE PILE OF CLOTHING IN FRONT OF ME STARTED TO MOVE AND TO MUMBLE.

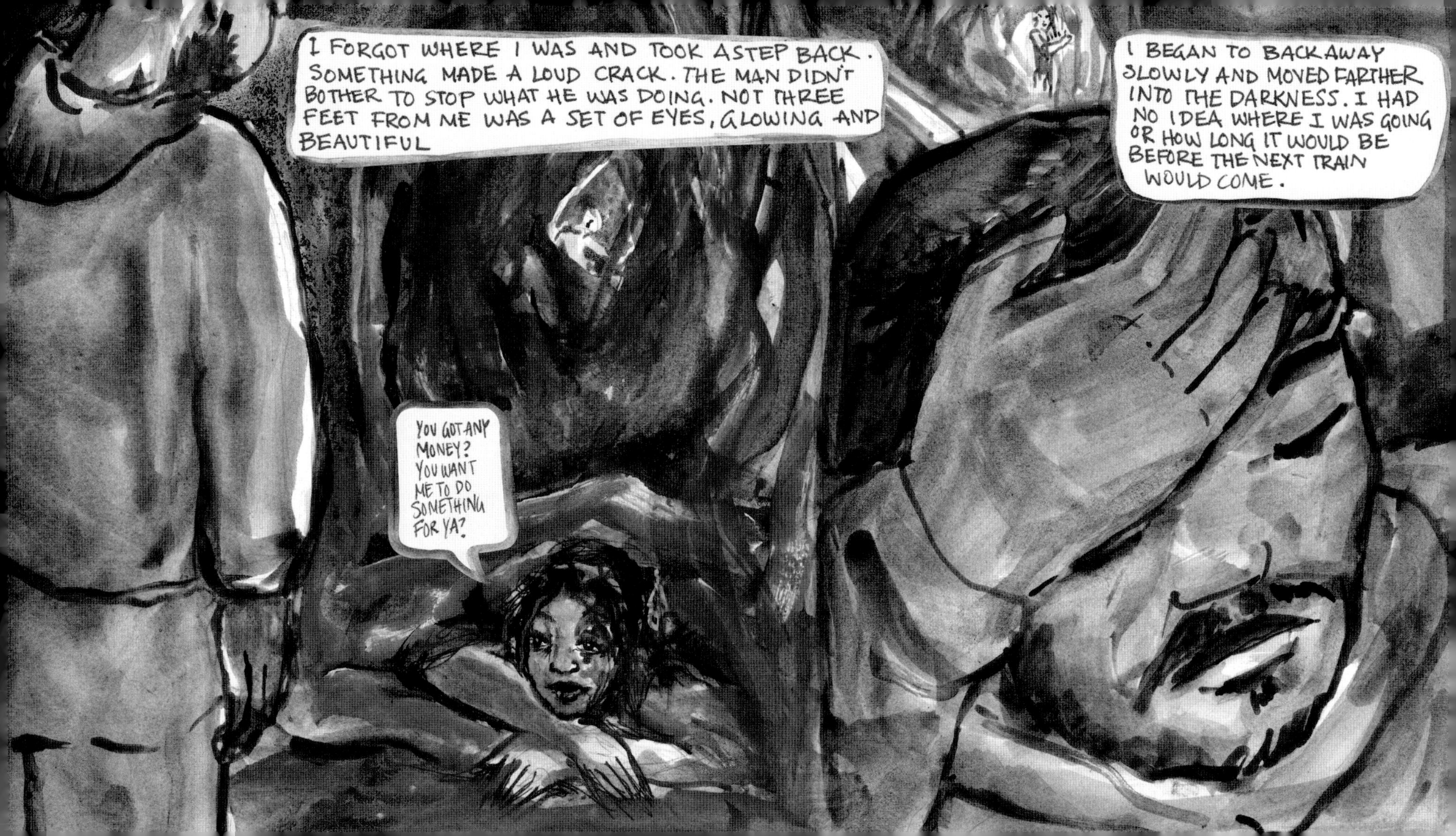
I FORGOT WHERE I WAS AND TOOK A STEP BACK. SOMETHING MADE A LOUD CRACK. THE MAN DIDN'T BOTHER TO STOP WHAT HE WAS DOING. NOT THREE FEET FROM ME WAS A SET OF EYES, GLOWING AND BEAUTIFUL
YOU GOT ANY MONEY? YOU WANT ME TO DO SOMETHING FOR YA?
I BEGAN TO BACK AWAY SLOWLY AND MOVED FARTHER INTO THE DARKNESS. I HAD NO IDEA WHERE I WAS GOING OR HOW LONG IT WOULD BE BEFORE THE NEXT TRAIN WOULD COME.

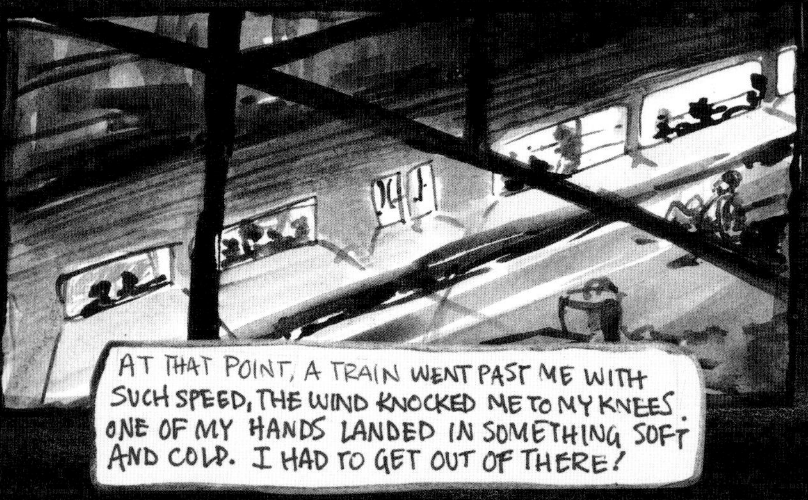
AT THAT POINT, A TRAIN WENT PAST ME WITH SUCH SPEED, THE WIND KNOCKED ME TO MY KNEES. ONE OF MY HANDS LANDED IN SOMETHING SOFT AND COLD. I HAD TO GET OUT OF THERE!

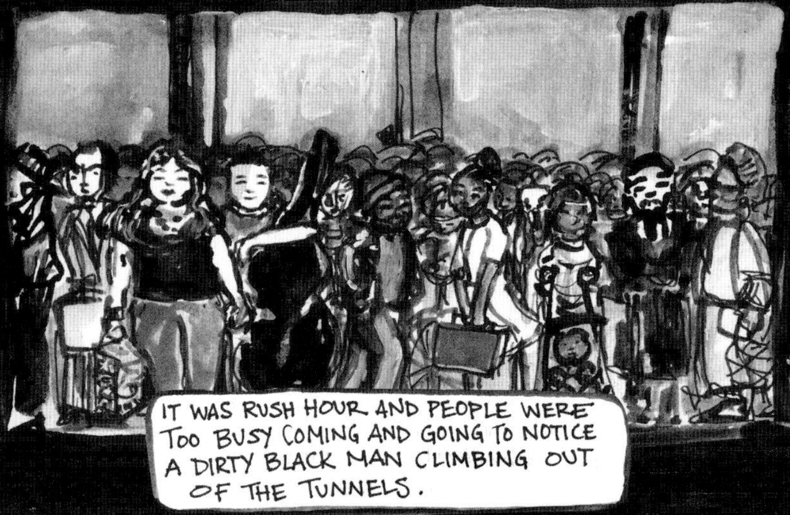
IT WAS RUSH HOUR AND PEOPLE WERE TOO BUSY COMING AND GOING TO NOTICE A DIRTY BLACK MAN CLIMBING OUT OF THE TUNNELS.

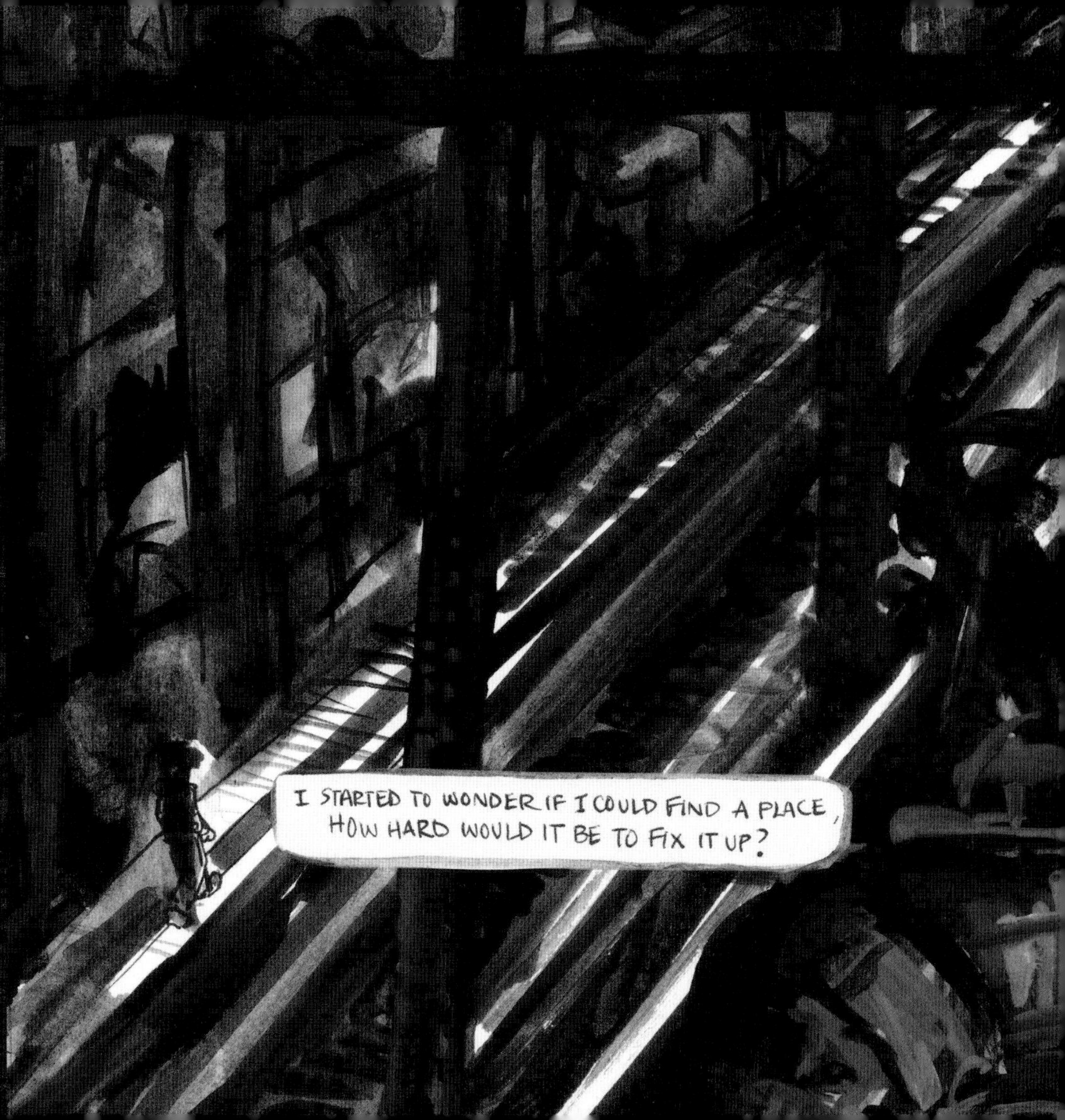
I STARTED TO WONDER IF I COULD FIND A PLACE, HOW HARD WOULD IT BE TO FIX IT UP?

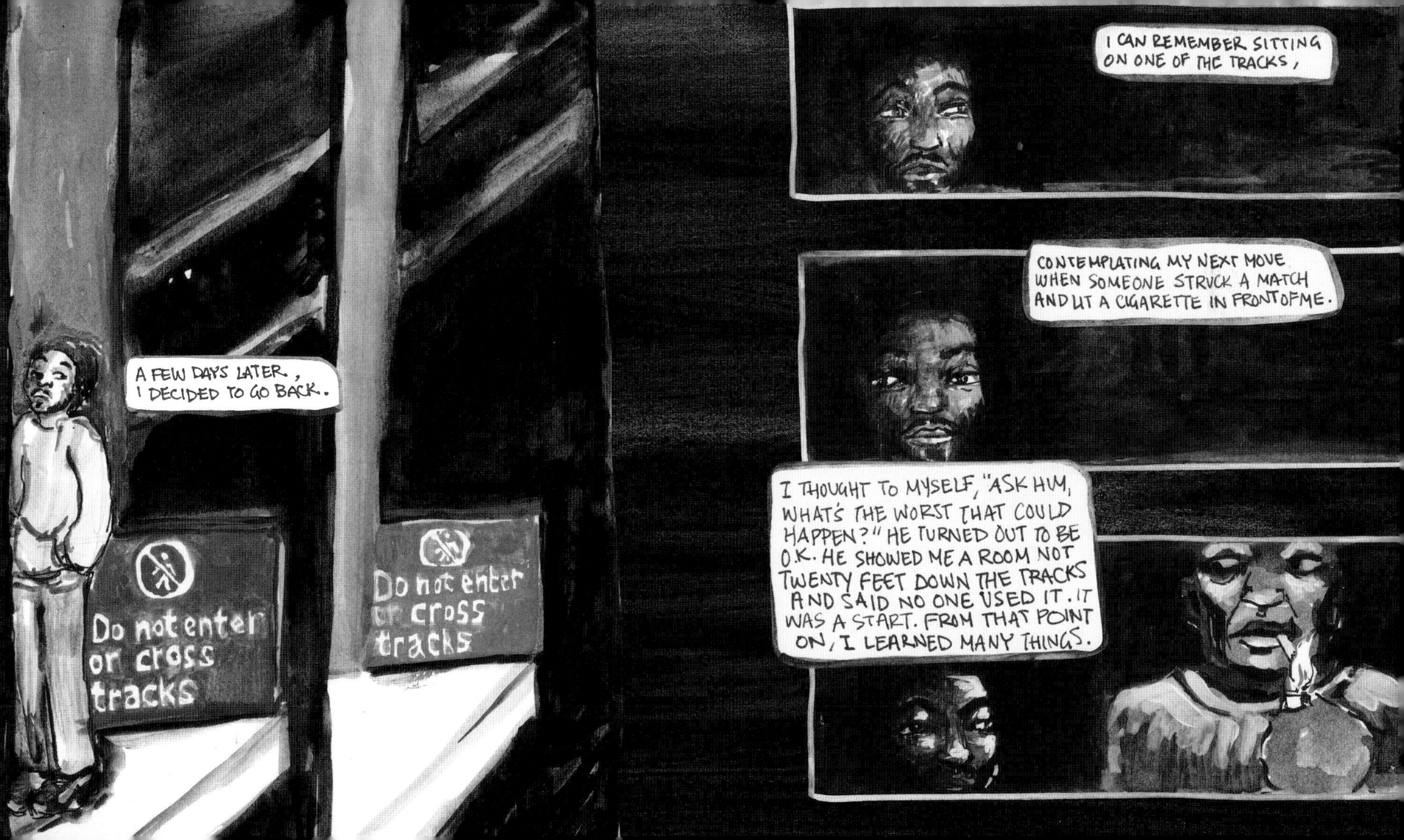
A FEW DAYS LATER, I DECIDED TO GO BACK.
Do not enter or cross tracks
Do not enter or cross tracks
I CAN REMEMBER SITTING ON ONE OF THE TRACKS,
CONTEMPLATING MY NEXT MOVE WHEN SOMEONE STRUCK A MATCH AND LIT A CIGARETTE IN FRONT OF ME.
I THOUGHT TO MYSELF, "ASK HIM, WHAT'S THE WORST THAT COULD HAPPEN?" HE TURNED OUT TO BE O.K. HE SHOWED ME A ROOM NOT TWENTY FEET DOWN THE TRACKS AND SAID NO ONE USED IT. IT WAS A START. FROM THAT POINT ON, I LEARNED MANY THINGS.

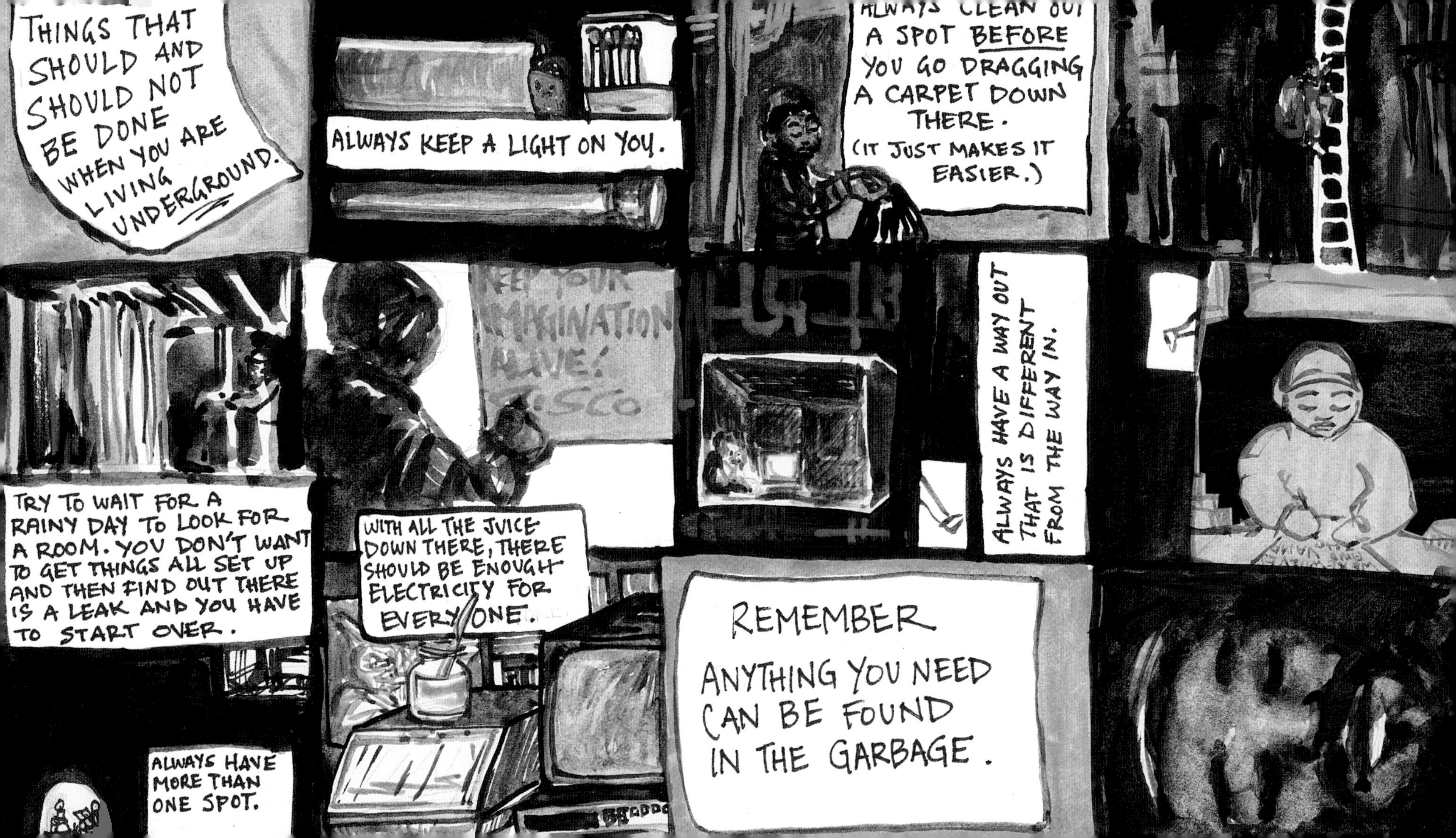
THINGS THAT SHOULD AND SHOULD NOT BE DONE WHEN YOU ARE LIVING UNDERGROUND.
ALWAYS KEEP A LIGHT ON YOU.
ALWAYS CLEAN OUT A SPOT BEFORE YOU GO DRAGGING A CARPET DOWN THERE.
(IT JUST MAKES IT EASIER.)
KEEP YOUR IMAGINATION ALIVE!
TRY TO WAIT FOR A RAINY DAY TO LOOK FOR A ROOM. YOU DON'T WANT TO GET THINGS ALL SET UP AND THEN FIND OUT THERE IS A LEAK AND YOU HAVE TO START OVER.
WITH ALL THE JUICE DOWN THERE, THERE SHOULD BE ENOUGH ELECTRICITY FOR EVERYONE.
ALWAYS HAVE A WAY OUT THAT IS DIFFERENT FROM THE WAY IN.
ALWAYS HAVE MORE THAN ONE SPOT.
REMEMBER
ANYTHING YOU NEED CAN BE FOUND IN THE GARBAGE.

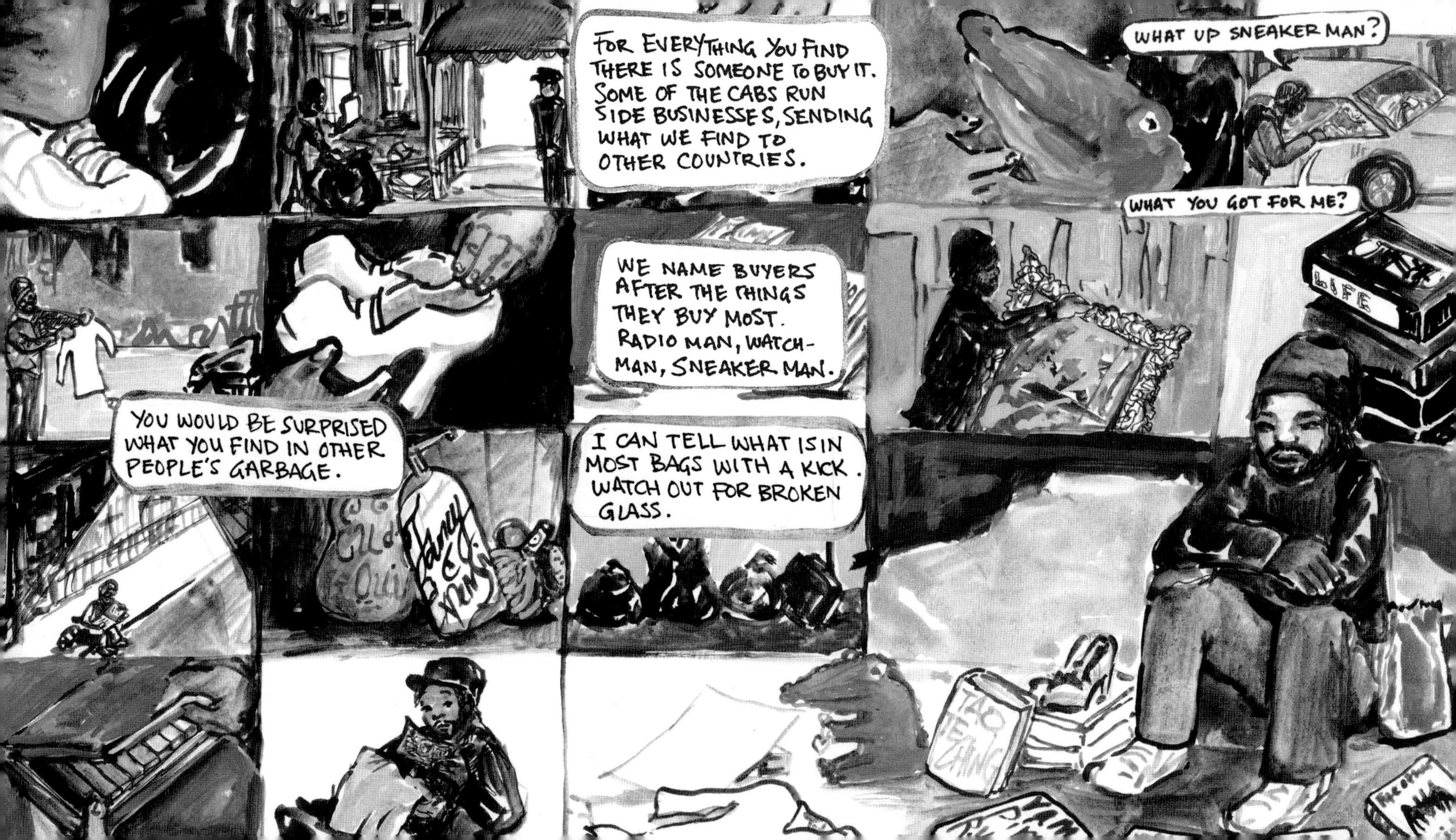

FOR EVERYTHING YOU FIND THERE IS SOMEONE TO BUY IT. SOME OF THE CABS RUN SIDE BUSINESSES, SENDING WHAT WE FIND TO OTHER COUNTRIES.
WHAT UP SNEAKER MAN?
WHAT YOU GOT FOR ME?
WE NAME BUYERS AFTER THE THINGS THEY BUY MOST. RADIO MAN, WATCH-MAN, SNEAKER MAN.
LIFE
YOU WOULD BE SURPRISED WHAT YOU FIND IN OTHER PEOPLE'S GARBAGE.
I CAN TELL WHAT IS IN MOST BAGS WITH A KICK. WATCH OUT FOR BROKEN GLASS.
TAO TE CHING

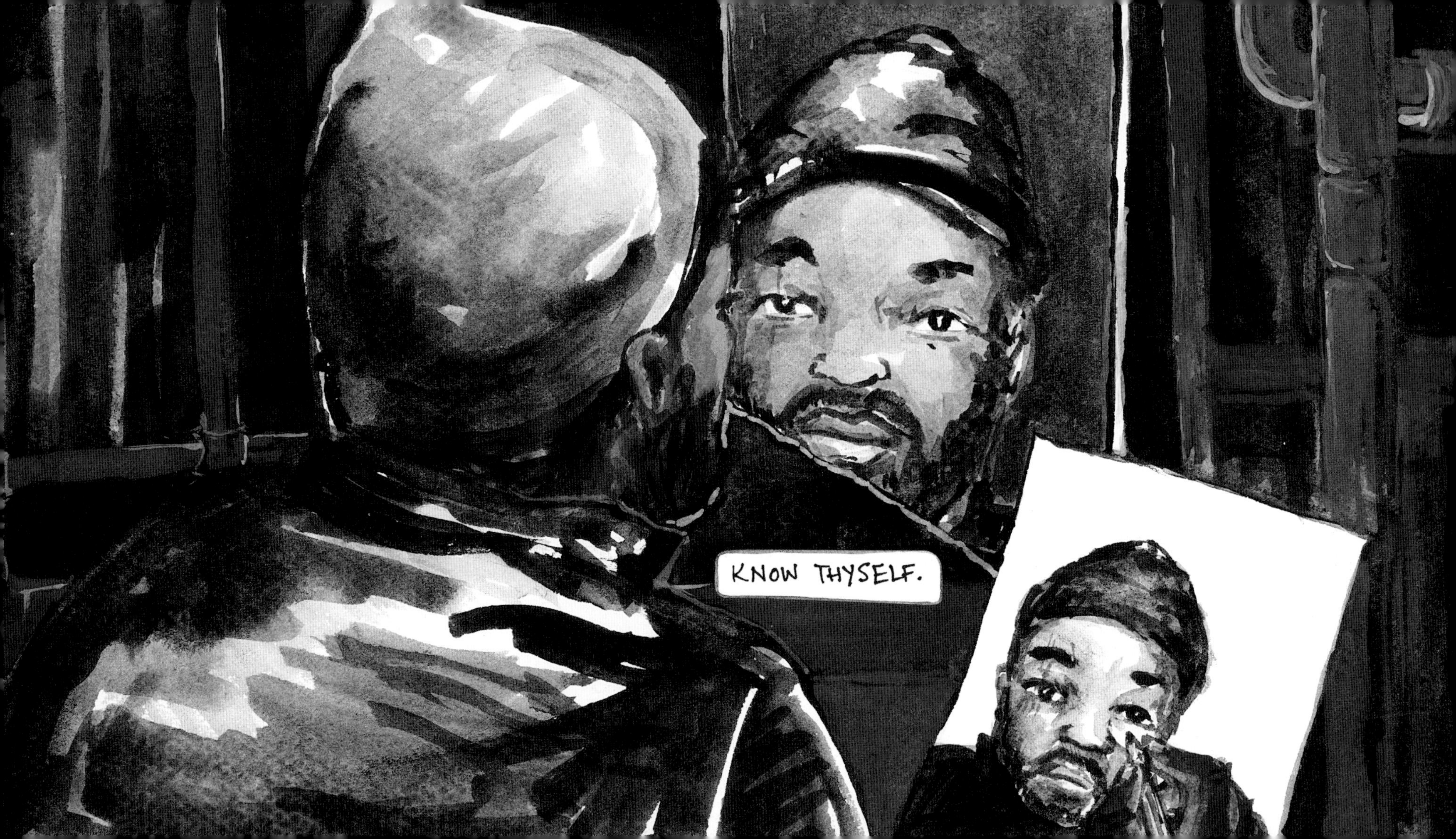
KNOW THYSELF.

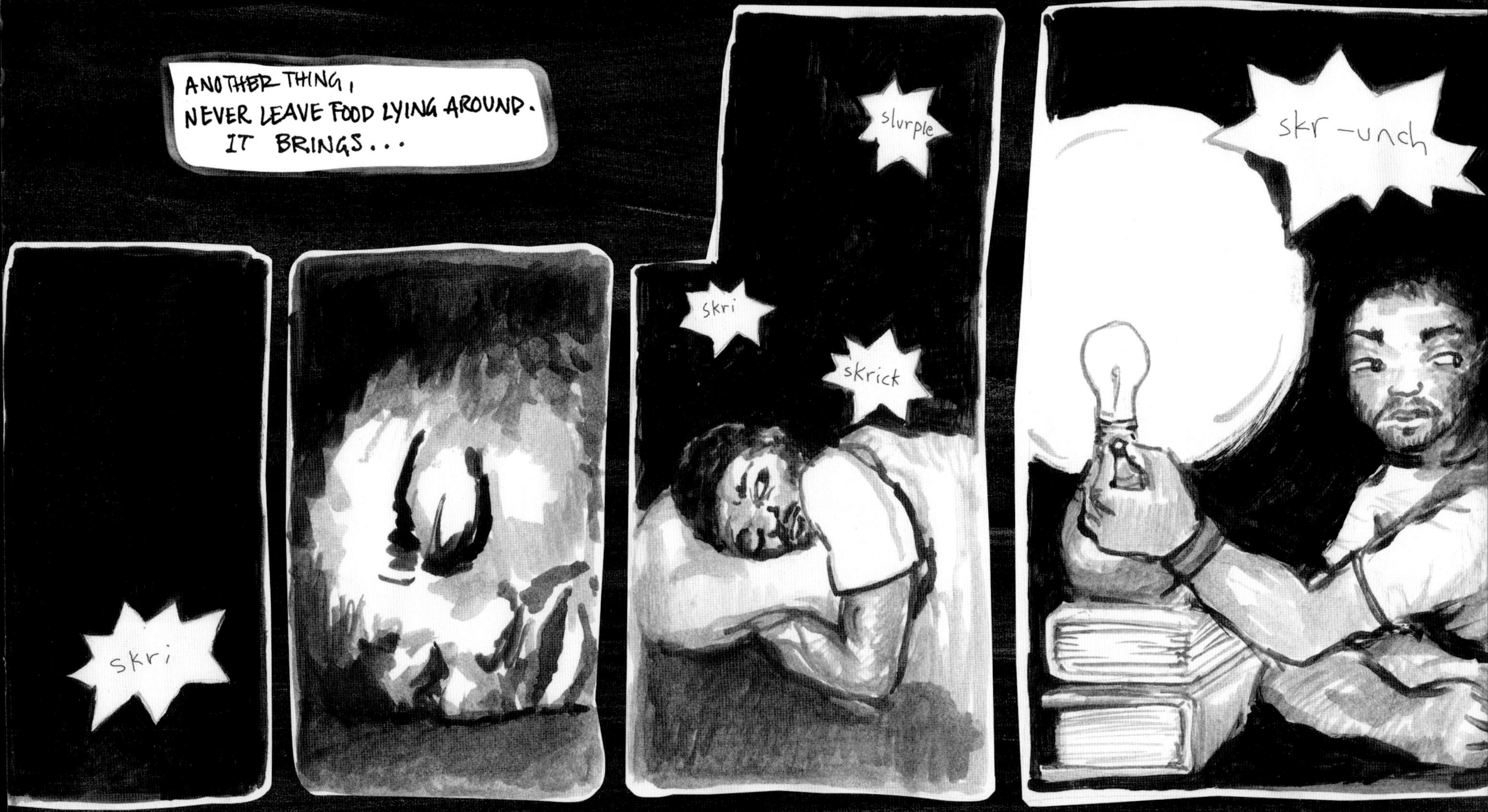
ANOTHER THING,
NEVER LEAVE FOOD LYING AROUND.
IT BRINGS...
skri
slurple
skri
skrick
skr-unch

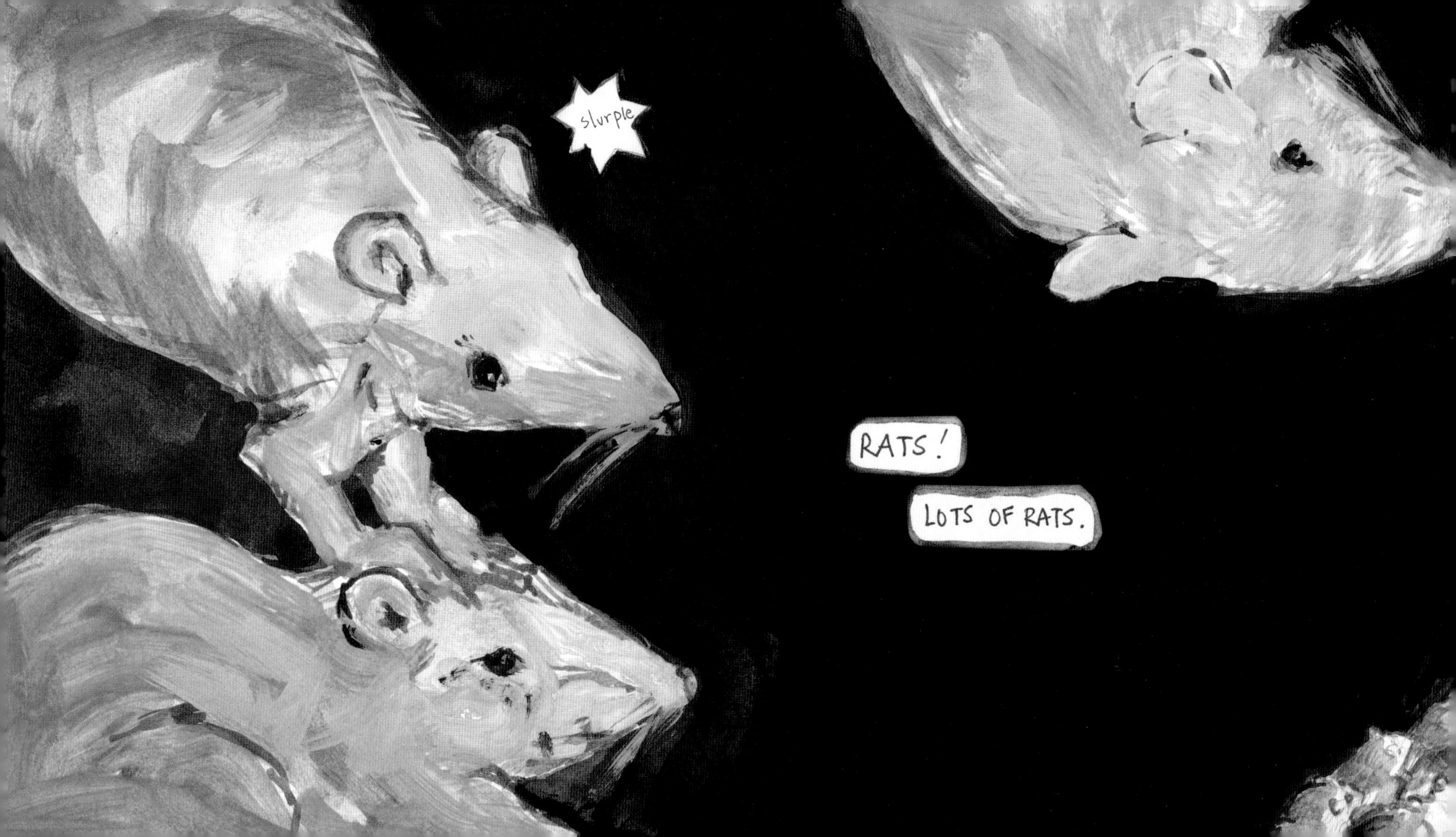
slurple
RATS!
LOTS OF RATS.

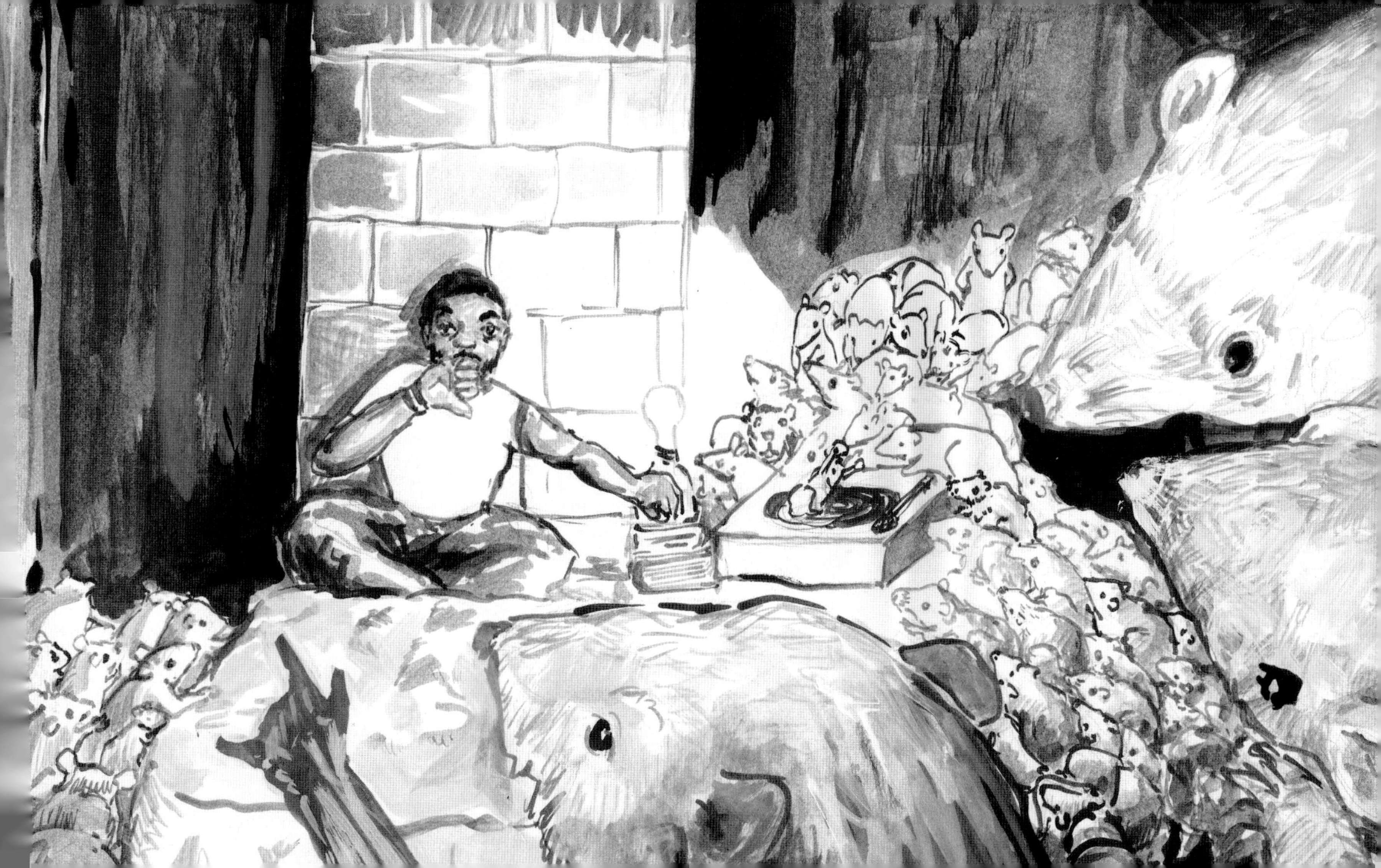

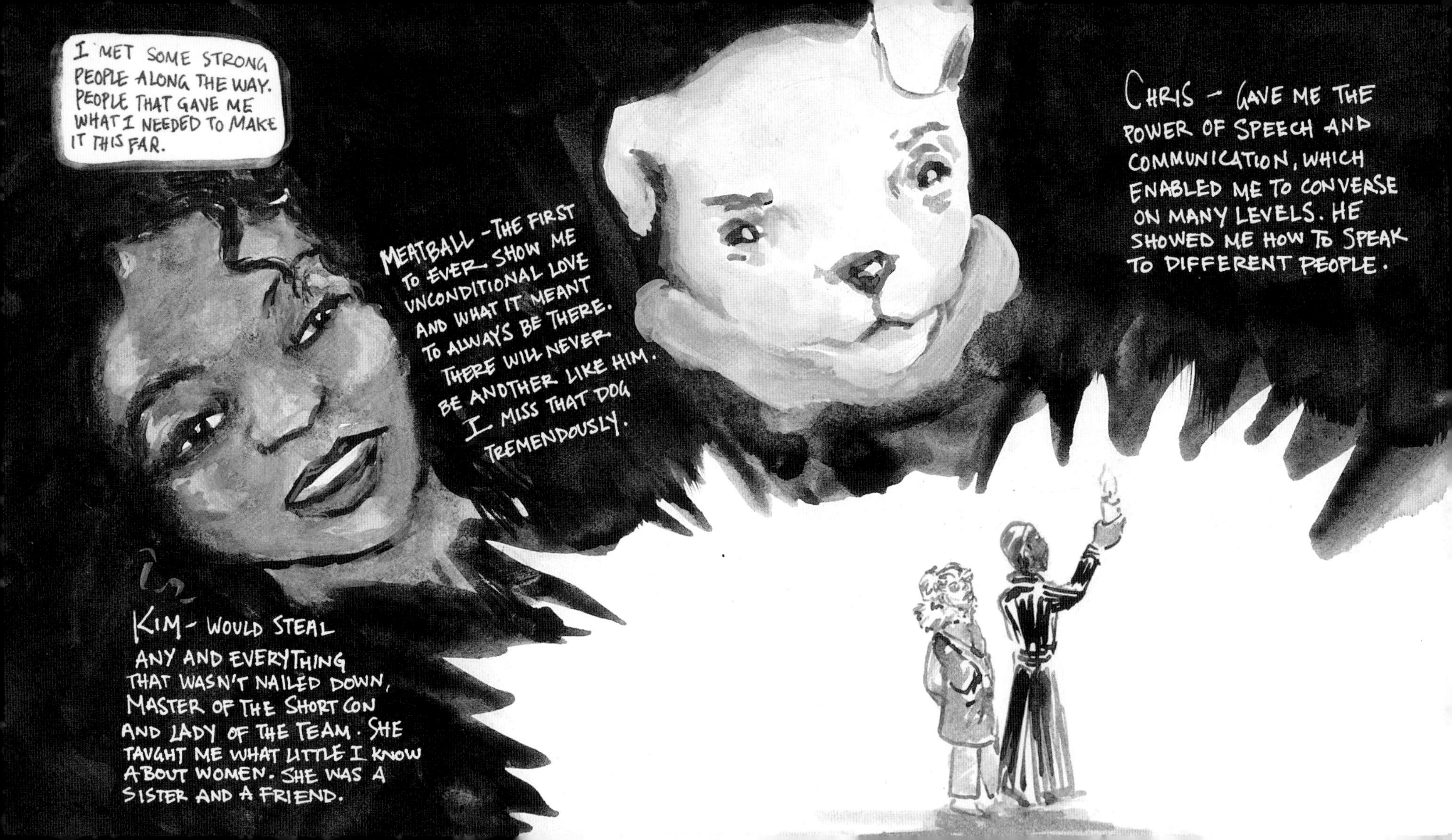
I MET SOME STRONG PEOPLE ALONG THE WAY. PEOPLE THAT GAVE ME WHAT I NEEDED TO MAKE IT THIS FAR.
KIM - WOULD STEAL ANY AND EVERYTHING THAT WASN'T NAILED DOWN, MASTER OF THE SHORT CON AND LADY OF THE TEAM. SHE TAUGHT ME WHAT LITTLE I KNOW ABOUT WOMEN. SHE WAS A SISTER AND A FRIEND.
MEATBALL - THE FIRST TO EVER SHOW ME UNCONDITIONAL LOVE AND WHAT IT MEANT TO ALWAYS BE THERE. THERE WILL NEVER BE ANOTHER LIKE HIM. I MISS THAT DOG TREMENDOUSLY.
CHRIS - GAVE ME THE POWER OF SPEECH AND COMMUNICATION, WHICH ENABLED ME TO CONVERSE ON MANY LEVELS. HE SHOWED ME HOW TO SPEAK TO DIFFERENT PEOPLE.

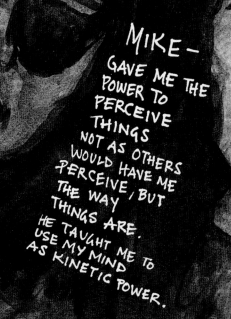

MIKE—
GAVE ME THE
POWER TO
PERCEIVE
THINGS
NOT AS OTHERS
WOULD HAVE ME
PERCEIVE, BUT
THE WAY
THINGS ARE.
HE TAUGHT ME TO
USE MY MIND
AS KINETIC POWER.

JORDAN—
WAS LIKE THE
BROTHER I NEVER
HAD. WITH ENOUGH
BOOK SMARTS FOR
EVERY ONE ON THE
LOWER EAST SIDE.
HE SHOWED
ME WHAT
LITERATURE CAN
BE WORTH. IN THE
RIGHT HANDS. ONE
BOOK MIGHT MEAN NOTHING
TO ONE PERSON, BUT TO
SOMEONE ELSE,
IT COULD CHANGE
THEIR WORLD.

PEOPLE I'LL NEVER FORGET.
I AM IN DEBT TO ALL OF THEM
BECAUSE TODAY I AM ALL OF THEM.

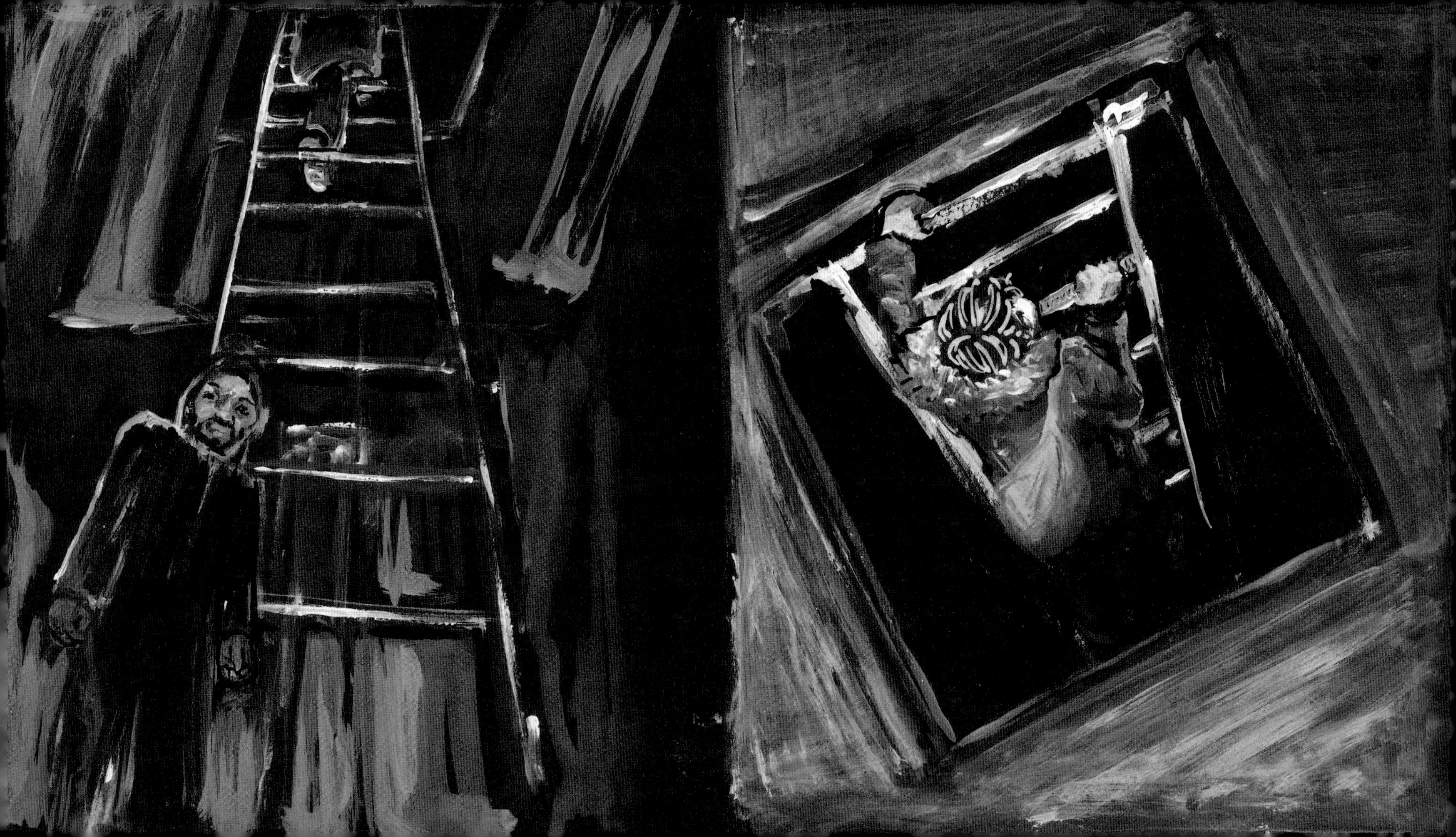

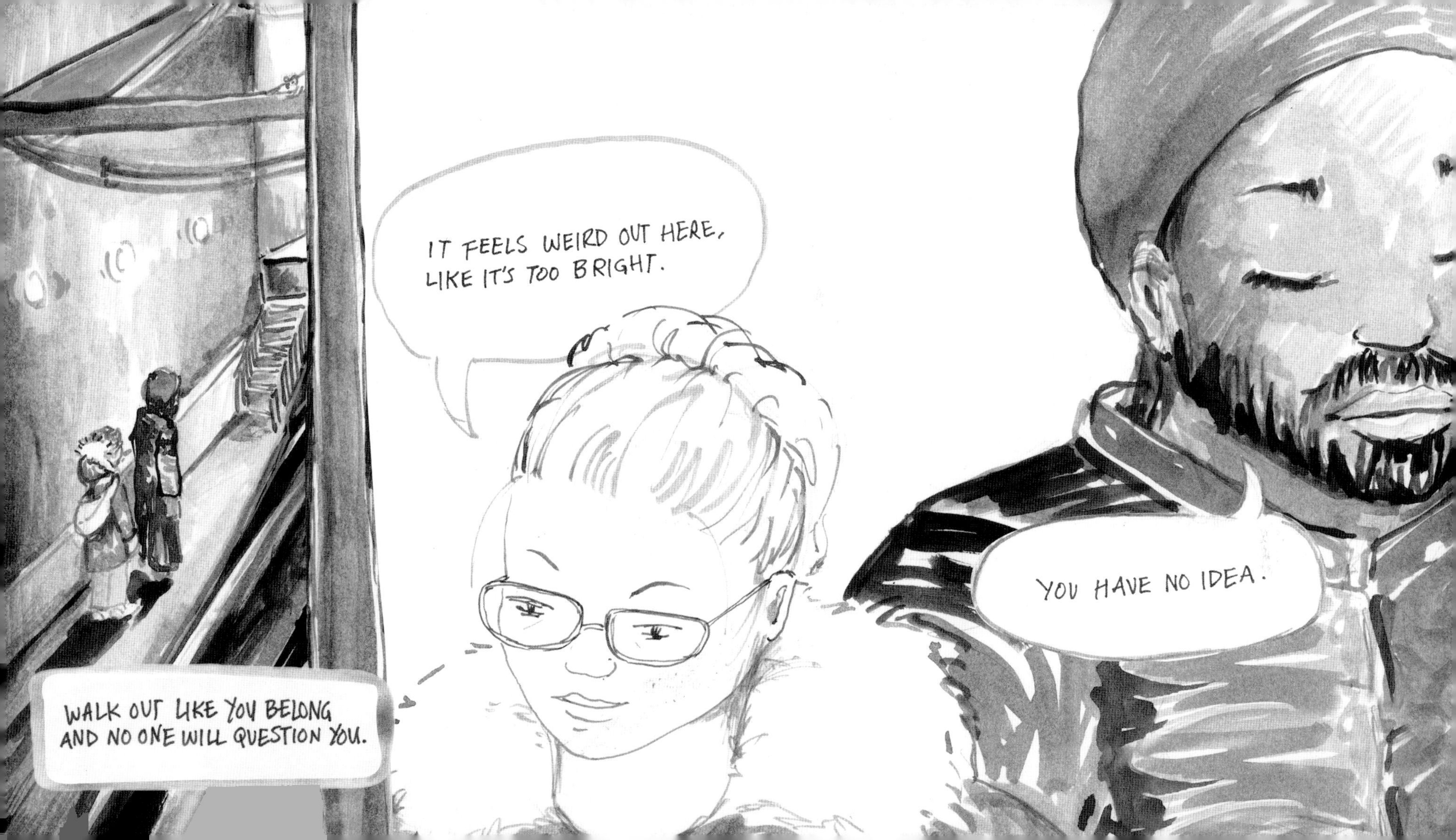
WALK OUT LIKE YOU BELONG AND NO ONE WILL QUESTION YOU.
IT FEELS WEIRD OUT HERE, LIKE IT'S TOO BRIGHT.
YOU HAVE NO IDEA.

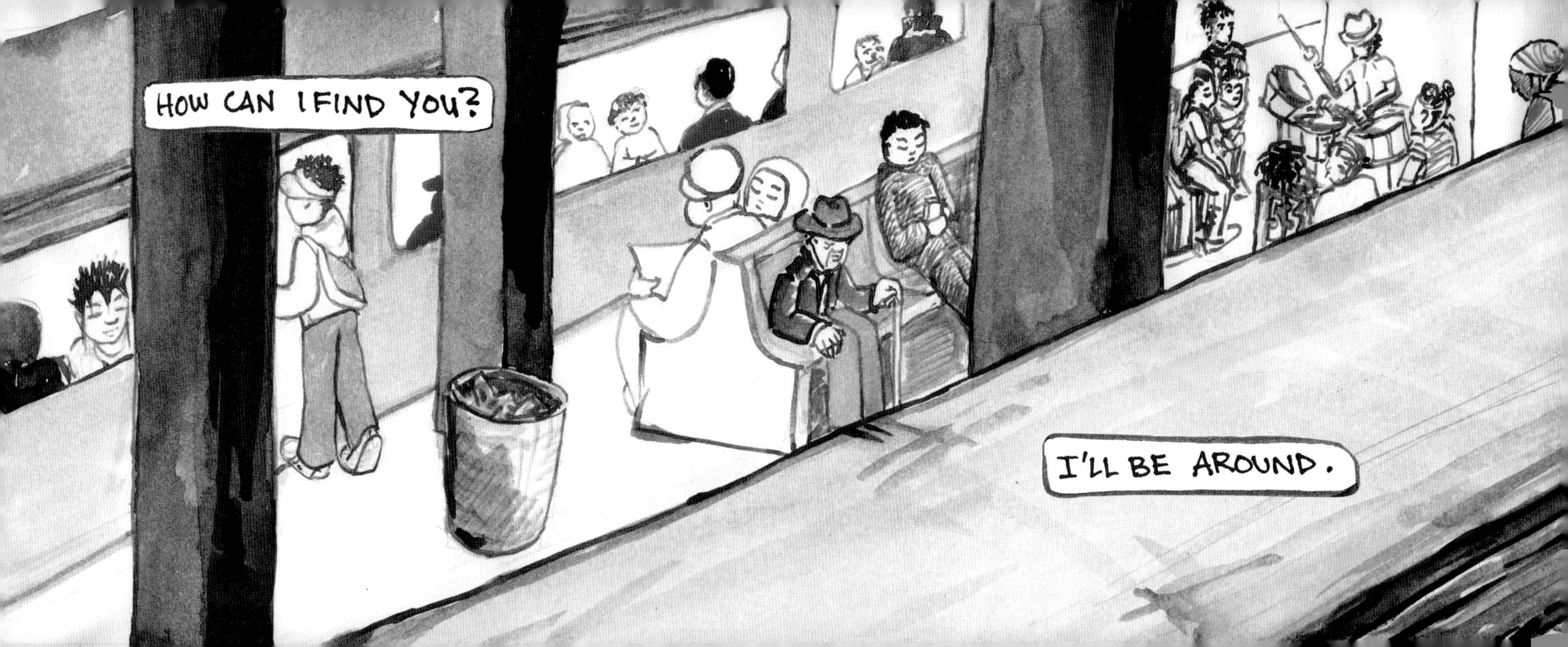
HOW CAN I FIND YOU?
I'LL BE AROUND.

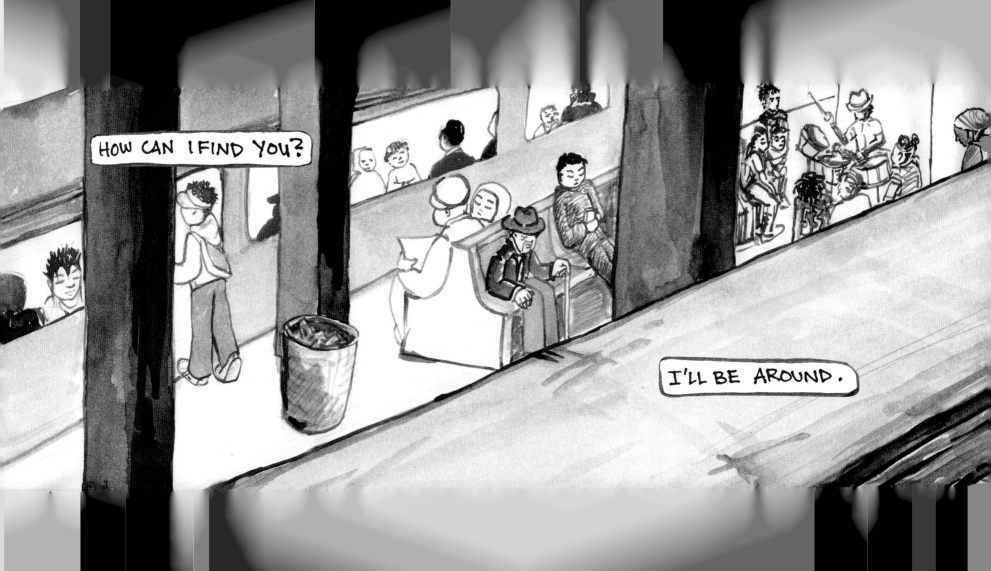

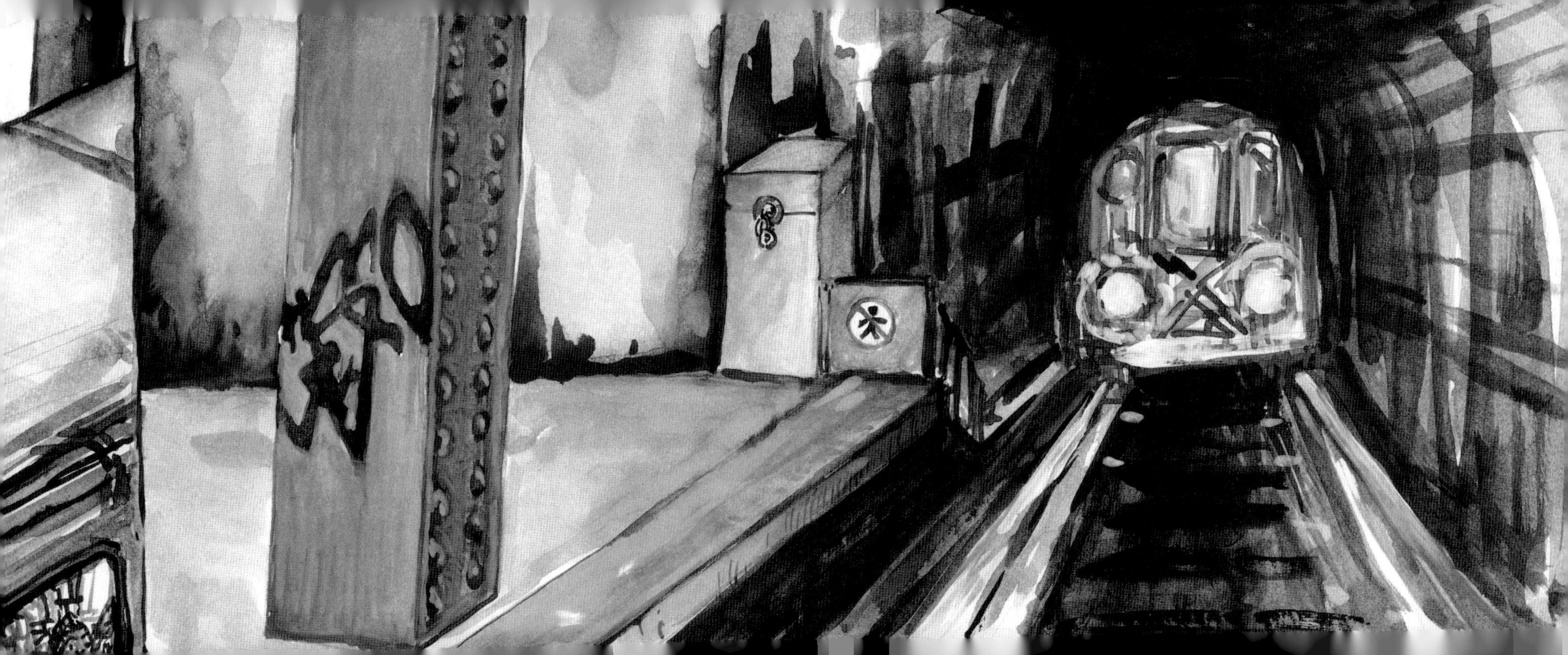

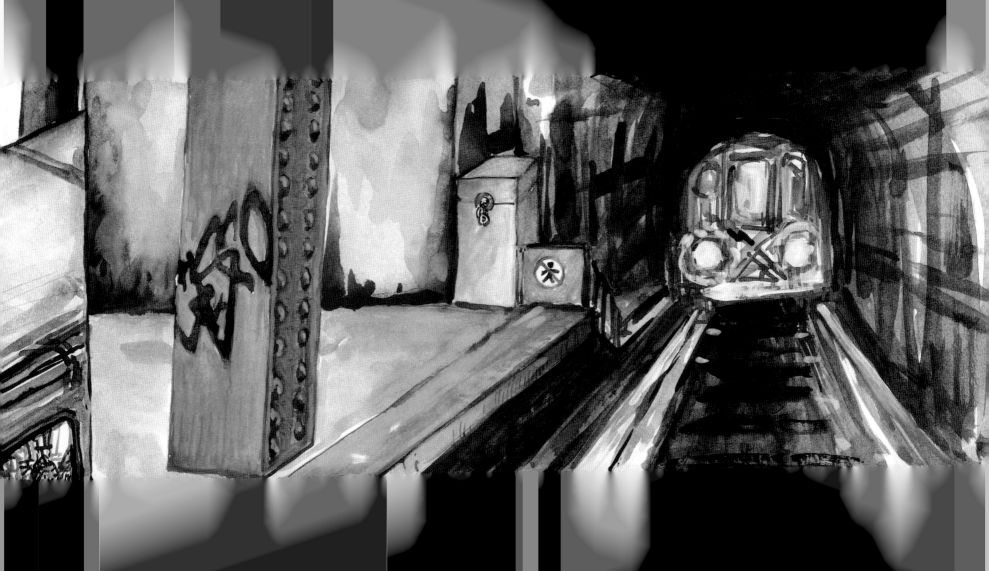

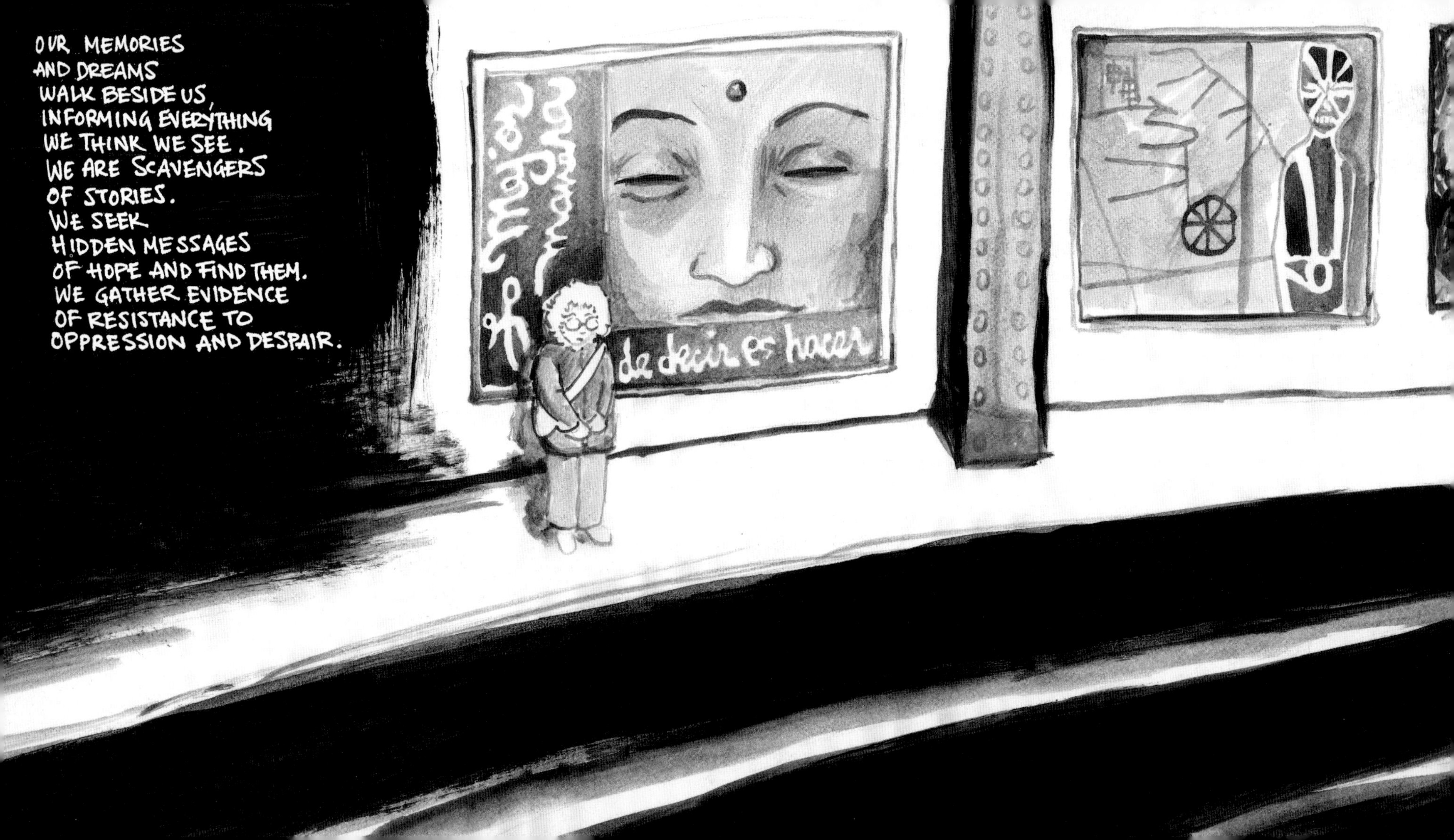
OUR MEMORIES
AND DREAMS
WALK BESIDE US,
INFORMING EVERYTHING
WE THINK WE SEE.
WE ARE SCAVENGERS
OF STORIES.
WE SEEK
HIDDEN MESSAGES
OF HOPE AND FIND THEM.
WE GATHER EVIDENCE
OF RESISTANCE TO
OPPRESSION AND DESPAIR.
de decir es hacer

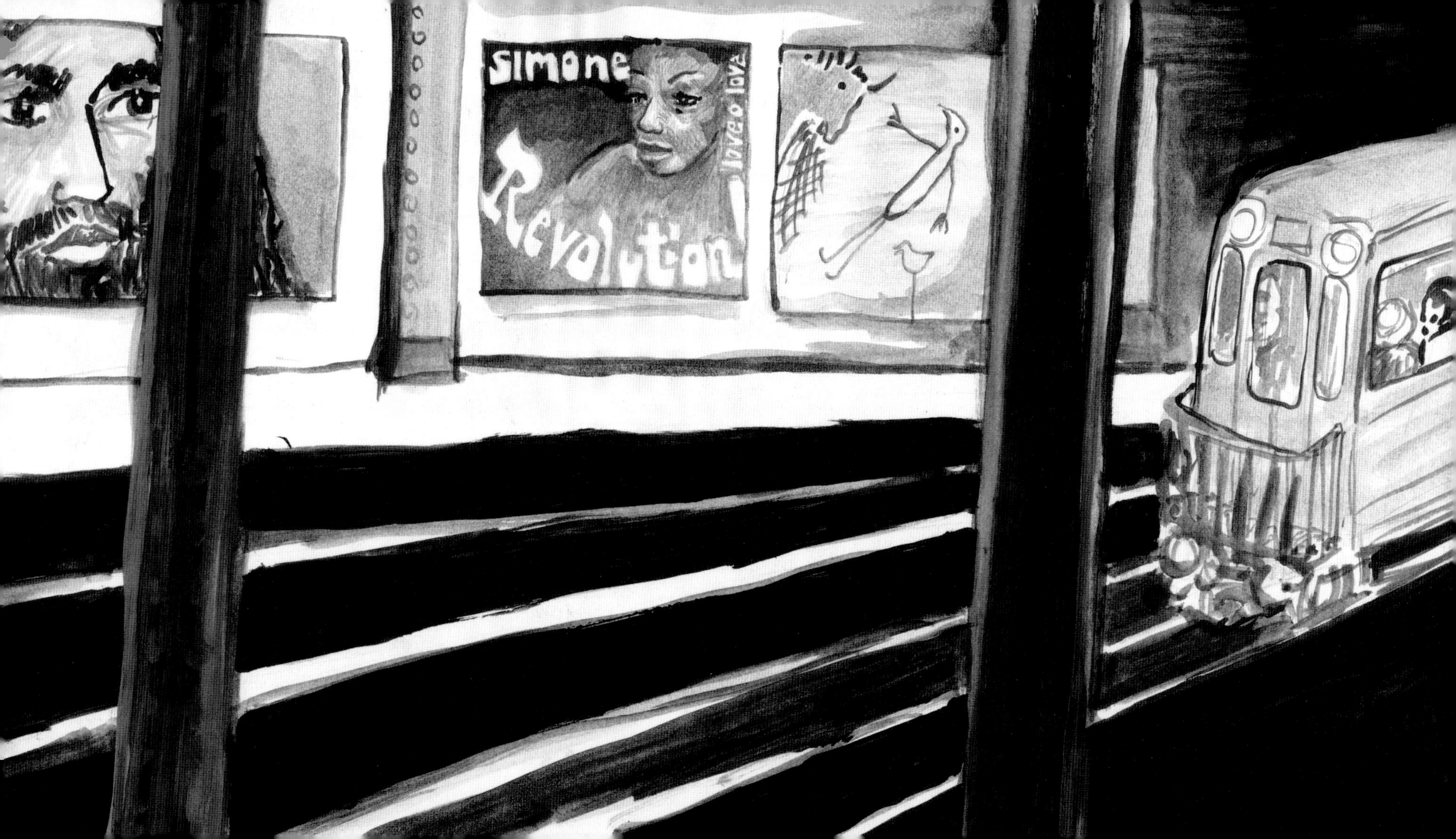

Simone
Revolution
love o love

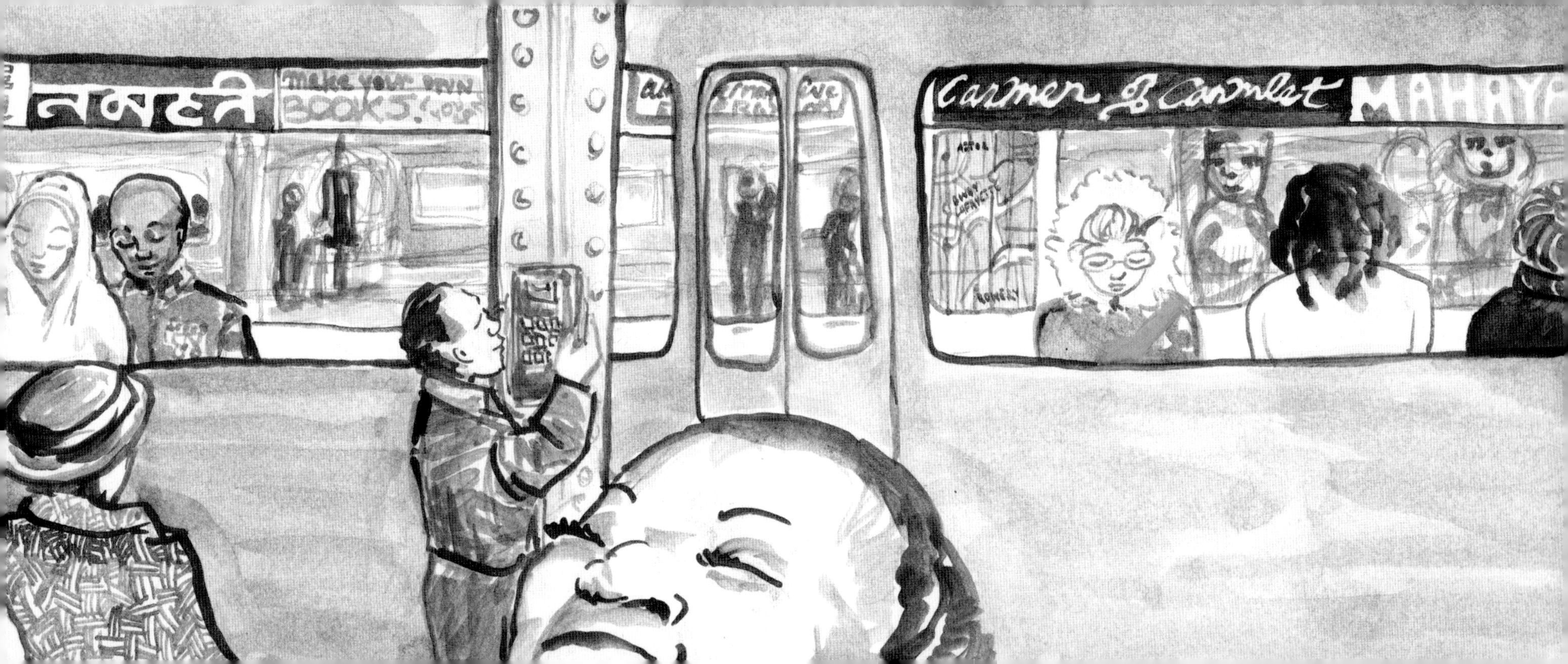
make your own
BOOKS!
Carmen of Camelot
ASTOR
BWAY LAFAYETTE
BOWERY

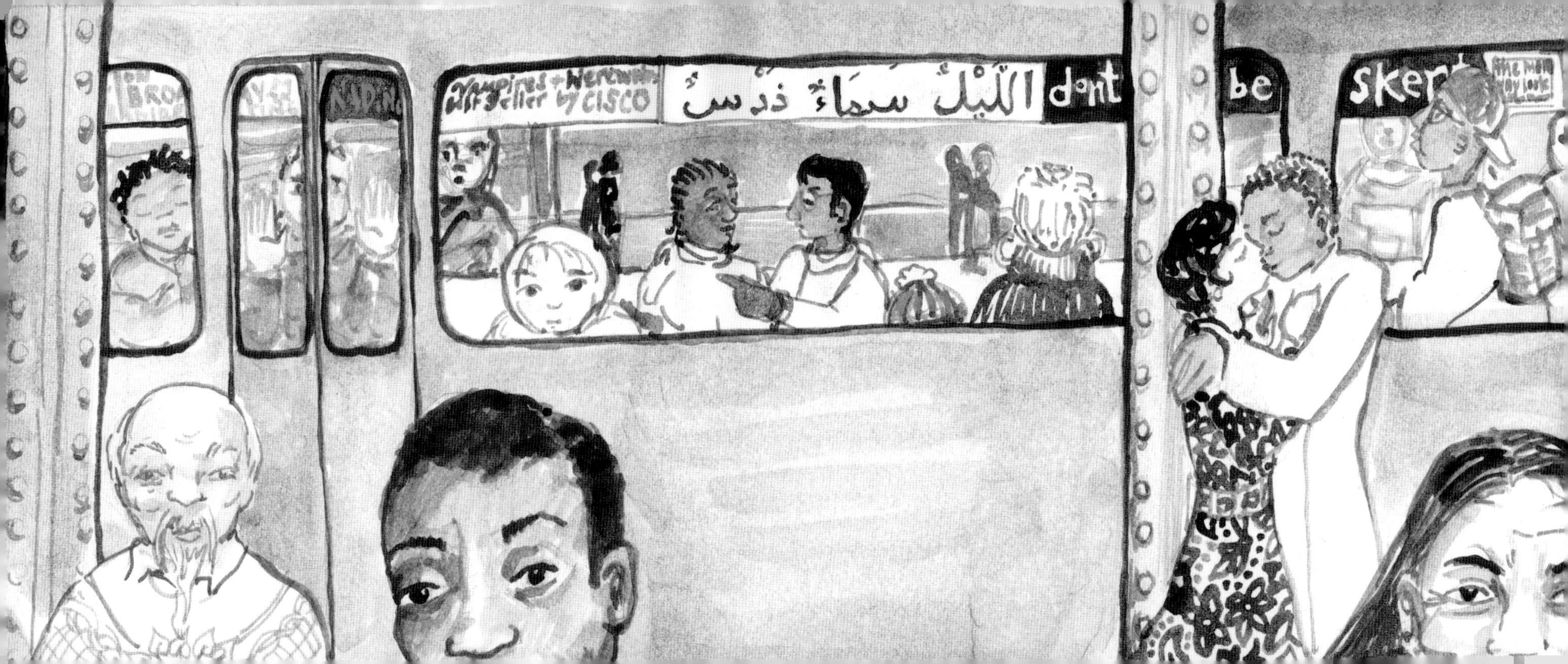
by CISCO
dont
be

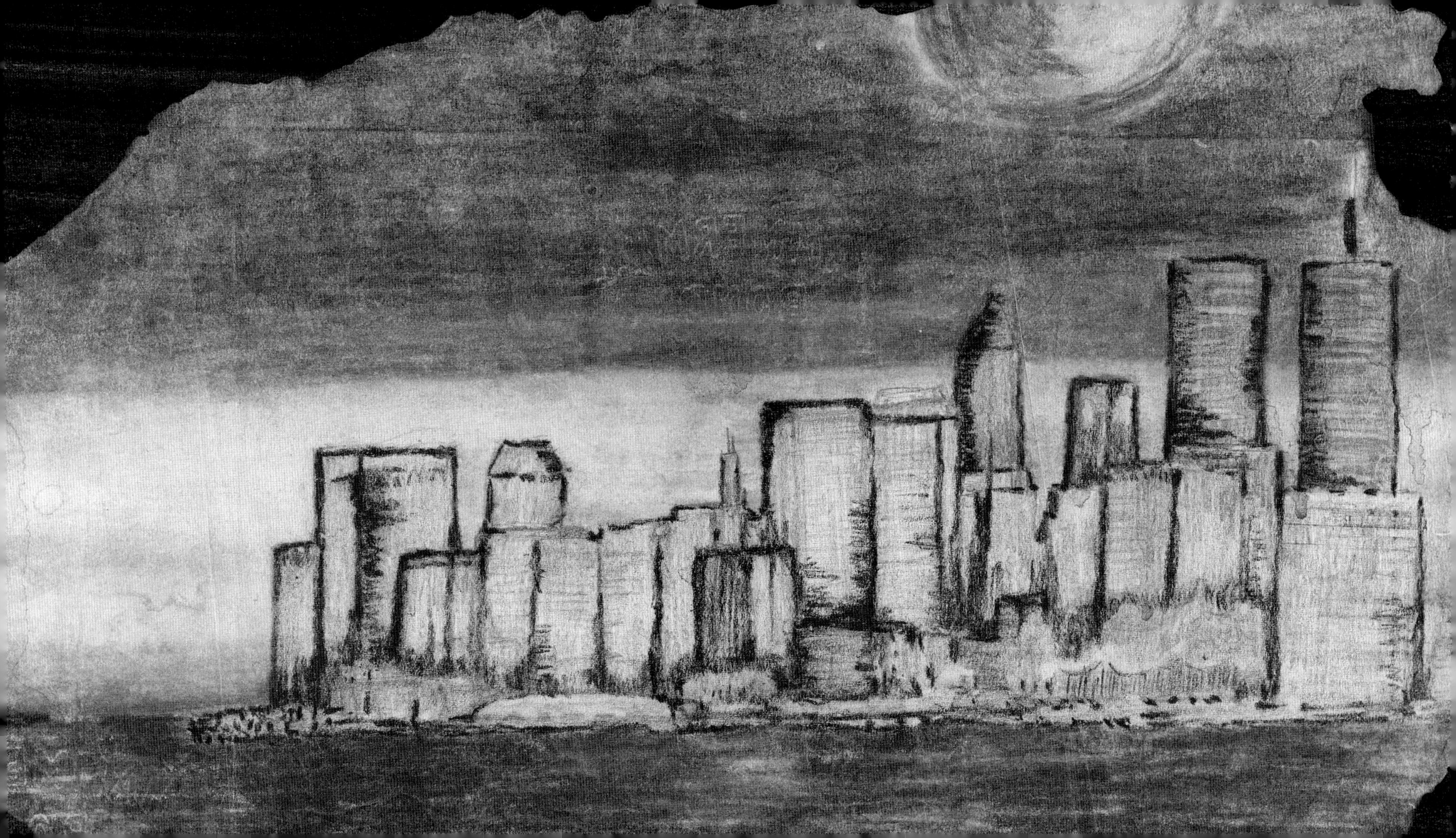

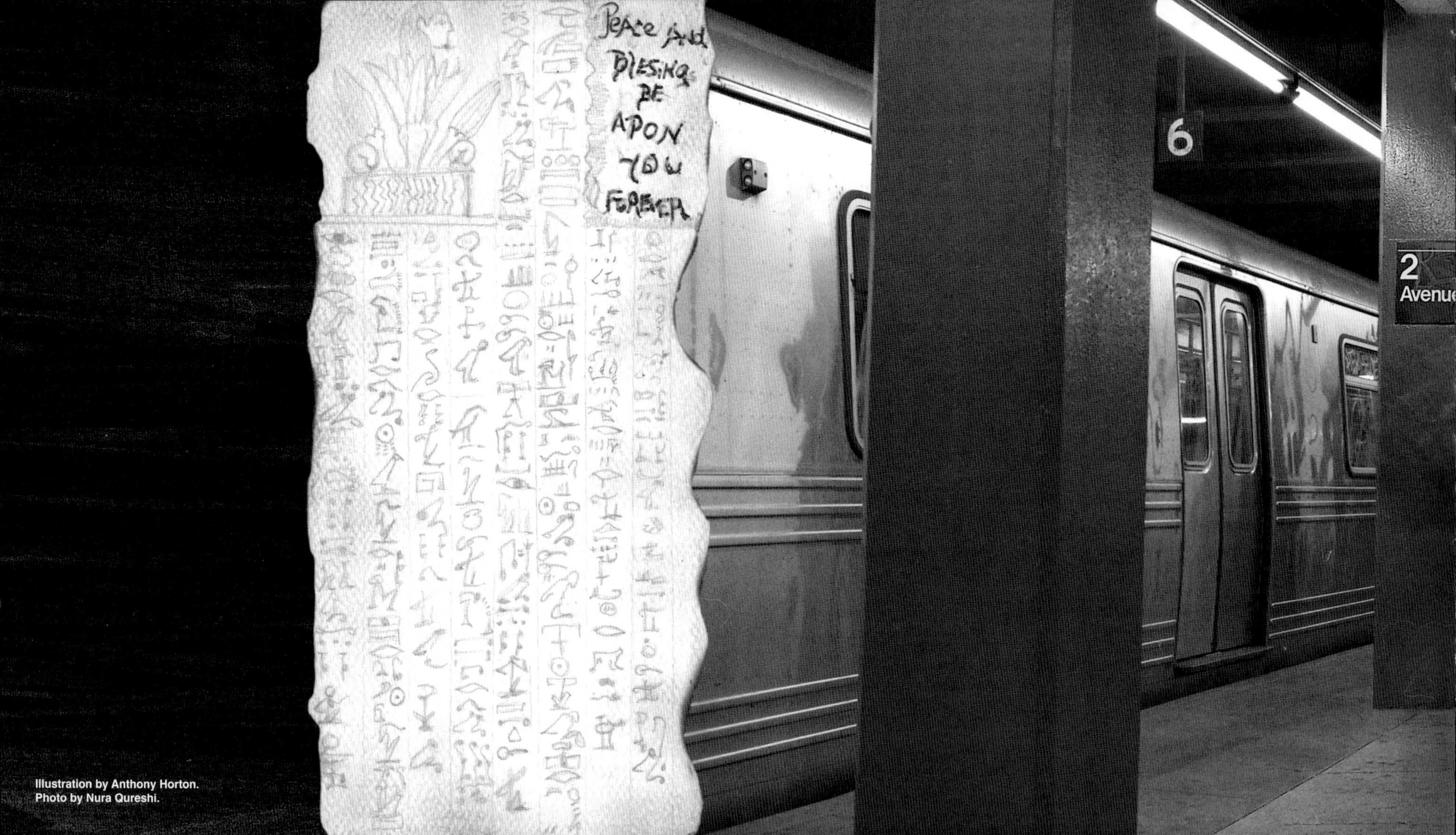

Peace And Blesings Be Apon You Forever
6
2
Avenue

Illustration by Anthony Horton.
Photo by Nura Qureshi.

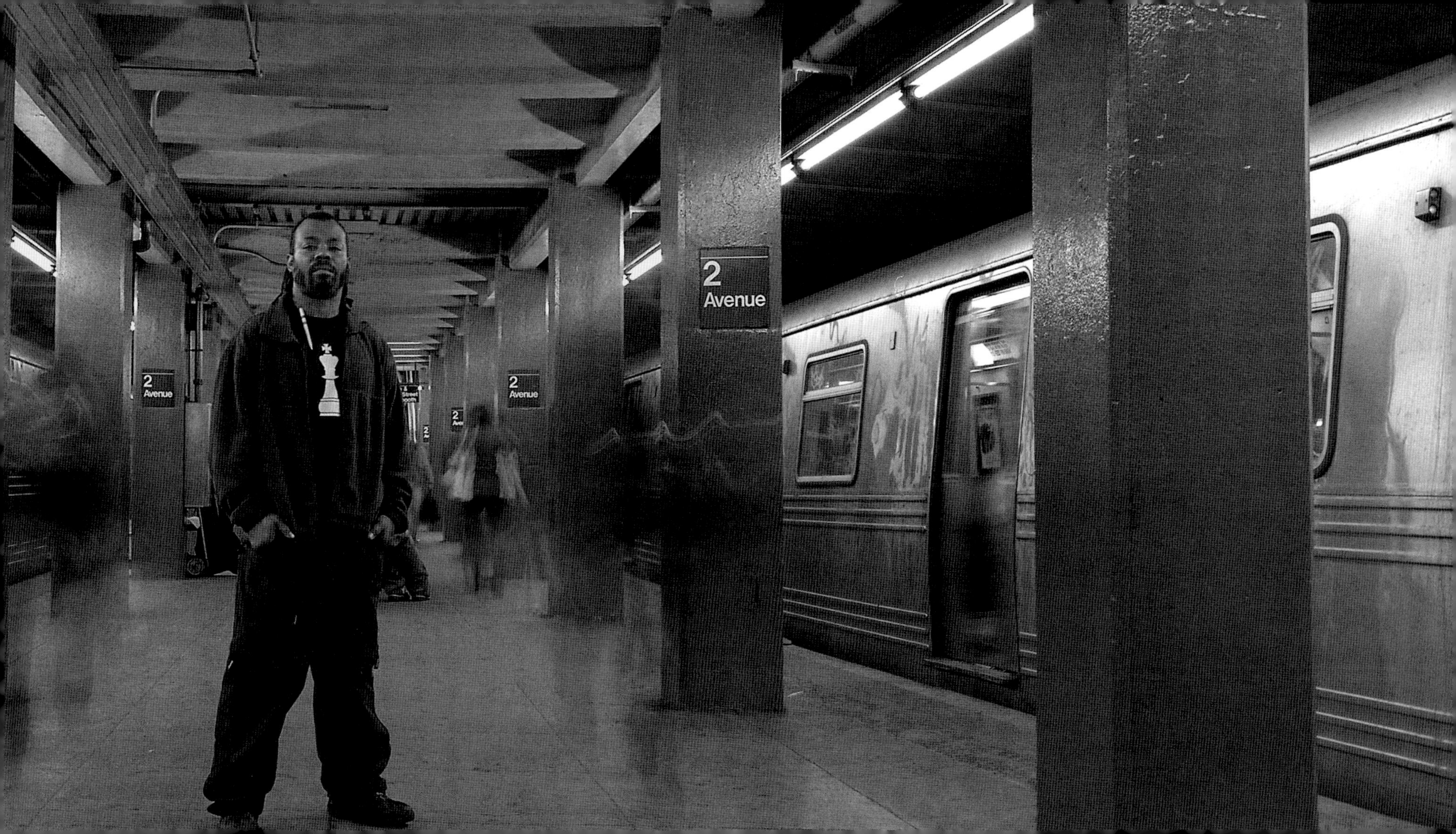
2
Avenue

DEDICATED TO LOVE

for our Grandparents

THANK YOU
DR. MILTON LANDOWNE
DR. WILLIAM H. TIMBERLAKE
YELLOW DOOR STUDIO
CANNONBALL PRESS
CISCO, ALL THE FOLKS
WHO STAYED WITH US IN
THE TOMBS AND THOSE
WHO GOT US OUT, Lisandro + MARY
♡ MAHAYANA, DAVID, EDITH ♡, NORA
CAT AND CHARLOTTE, MOLLY AND DOM, MALI
VIN, KHAN, KYRON, SHOGO, BOIVERT
PAT SIMPSON, KHALIL,
GROUNDSWELL and THE
FOUNDATIONS OF NEW YORK CITY.

 For information, write Cinco Puntos Press, 701 Texas, El Paso, TX 79901 or call at (915) 838-1625. Printed in the United States.
FIRST EDITION 1 0 9 8 7 6 5 4 3 2 1
Library of Congress Cataloging-in-Publication Data. Youme. Pitch black / by Youme Landowne and Anthony Horton. p. cm. ISBN 978-1-933693-06-4 1. Horton, Anthony, 1968—Comic books, strips, etc. 2. Homeless persons—New York (State)—New York—Biography—Comic books, strips, etc. 3. Homeless persons as artists—New York (State)—New York—Biography—Comic books, strips, etc. 4. Homelessness—New York (State)—New York—Comic books, strips, etc. 5. Subways—Social aspects—New York (State)—New York—Comic books, strips, etc. I. Horton, Anthony, 1968– II. Title. HV4506 N7Y68 2007 305.38'96942092—dc22 [B] 2007019444

Endpapers and Cityscape by Anthony Horton
Book design by Little Lulu's mother, Anne M. Giangiulio
For Bubba and Lucia, my light — AMG

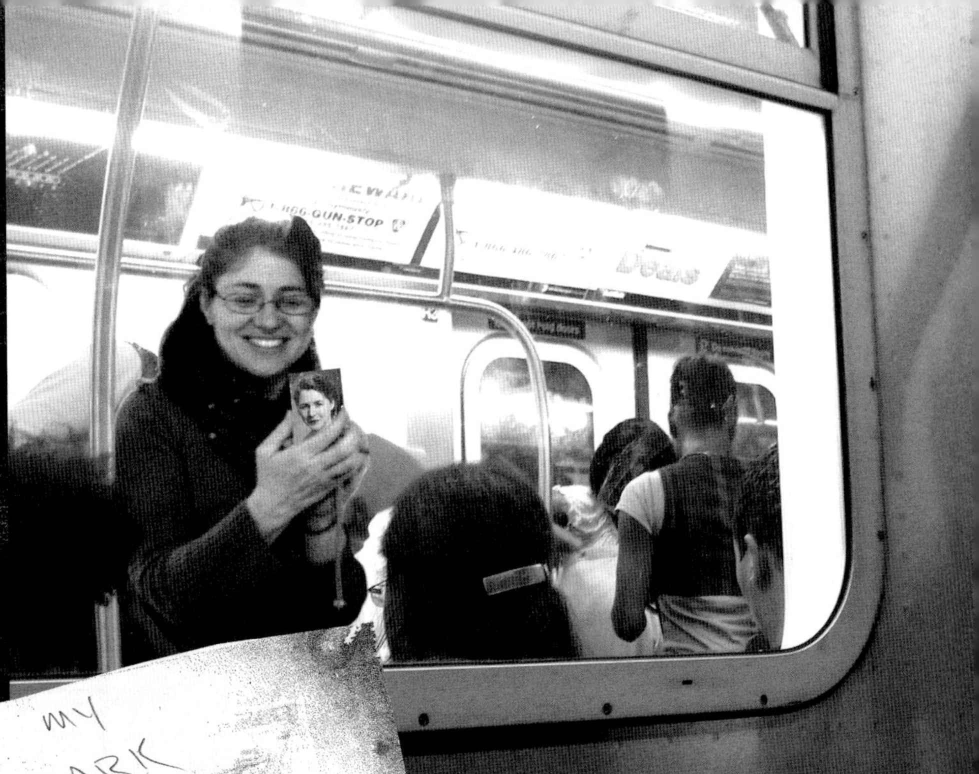
Photo by Youme Landowne

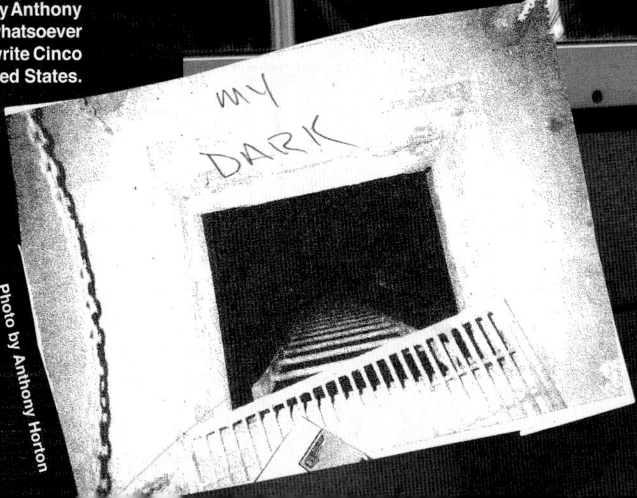
MY DARK
Photo by Anthony Horton

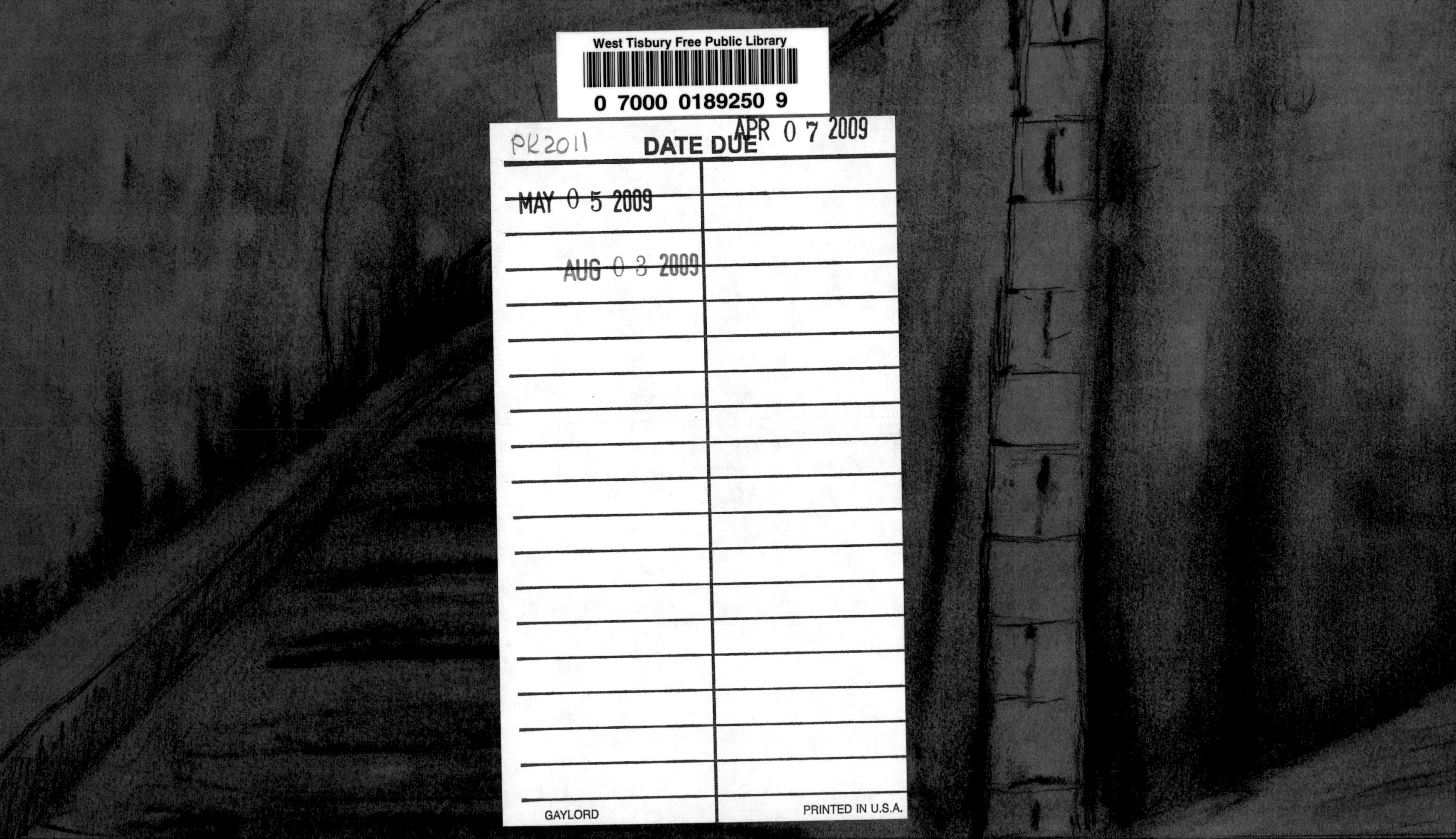